THERAPEUTIC ACTION

THERAPEUTIC ACTION

AN EARNEST PLEA FOR IRONY

Jonathan Lear

KARNAC
LONDON   NEW YORK

Copyright © 2003 by Jonathan Lear

Production Editor: Robert D. Hack
This book was set in 12 pt. New Baskerville by Alpha Graphics of Pittsfield, NH.

Published in UK 2003 by
H. Karnac (Books) Ltd.
6 Pembroke Buildings
London NW10 6RE

ISBN: 1 85575 994 2

Published in US by Other Press LLC.

Printed and bound in Great Britain by Biddles Ltd *www.biddles.co.uk*

www.karnacbooks.com

*This book is dedicated
to Jane and Richard Levin.*

It also needs to be said that the love of truth is no less a passion because it desires truth rather than some less elevated end. In our field, the love of truth cannot be isolated from the passion for truth to ourselves and truth in human relationships. In other fields, too, the scientist is filled with love for his object precisely in his most creative and "dispassionate" moments. Scientific detachment in its genuine form, far from excluding love, is based on it. In our work it can be truly said that in our best moments of dispassionate and objective analyzing we love our object, the patient, more than at any other time and are compassionate with his whole being.

Hans Loewald

From the fact that irony is present it does not follow that earnestness is excluded. That is something only assistant professors assume.

Johannes Climacus

Contents

1

Introduction

How might a conversation fundamentally change the structure of the human psyche? I am not concerned merely with a conversation that leads someone to change his or her beliefs—even a conversation that leads to massive change of beliefs. I can imagine myself living through a scientific revolution: I am in college in Galileo's time; I'm taking Astronomy 101; indeed, Galileo is my professor! I come to understand the mathematics and the astronomy— and, whoosh!, I come to realize that the earth is not at the center of the universe. I can even imagine that my former beliefs were so strongly felt that, as I undergo this change, it is almost as if I can feel the earth under my feet move out to its orbit around the sun.[1] Still, this is not the kind of

---

1. Cp. Proust (1913)

Perhaps the immobility of things that surround us is forced upon them by our conviction that they are themselves and not anything

change I am talking about, though we are getting closer. For the psyche is in the business of adjusting and changing beliefs. Changing beliefs, being surprised about the change, reacting emotionally and feelingly toward it—this is just what the psyche does. Nothing about the psyche *itself* has to change in this process.

Imagine, though, someone who lived through the same scientific revolution and underwent the same changes of beliefs—but he did this unfeelingly. He used to think the earth was the center of the universe, now he no longer thinks the universe has a center. He can give reasons for his beliefs, even act as a teaching assistant in

---

else, by the immobility of our conception of them. For it always happened that when I awoke like this, and my mind struggled in an unsuccessful attempt to discover where I was, everything revolved around me through the darkness: things, places, years. My body, still too heavy with sleep to move, would endeavour to construe from the pattern of its tiredness the position of its various limbs, in order to deduce therefrom the direction of the wall, the location of the furniture, to piece together and give a name to the house in which it lay. Its memory, the composite memory of its ribs, its knees, its shoulder-blades, offered it a series of rooms in which it had at one time or another slept, while the unseen walls, shifting and adapting themselves to the shape of each successive room that it remembered, whirled around in the dark. And even before my brain, hesitating at the threshold of times and shapes, had reassembled the circumstances sufficiently to identify the room, it—my body—would recall from each room in succession the style of the bed, the position of the doors, the angle at which daylight came in at the windows, whether there was a passage outside, what I had had in my mind when I went to sleep and found there when I awoke. [Vol. 1, p. 5]

a course on the Copernican Revolution. But none of this means very much to him emotionally speaking. He is clever, his life is full of facts, the facts change, sometimes even a lot of facts change; but life itself is drab. Now imagine him undergoing some kind of conversation such that the outcome is that a new sense of vibrancy enters his life. He believes the same things, but he believes them differently. There is a newfound sense of wonder that humans could have thought this, amazement that the world could be *here* rather than *there*—even a sense of puzzlement, joy, and dread that it is no longer clear what "here" could mean.[2]

This does seem to be a fundamental change in the psyche. For the change is no longer merely in *what* the person believes, but in *how* he believes it. We are tempted to say that before the crucial conversation this person's belief-system was out of touch with his emotional life. He himself was cut off from his own sense of liveliness.

---

2. In his play *Jumpers*, Tom Stoppard (1972) has George, a philosophy professor, describe the following encounter: "Meeting a friend in a corridor, Wittgenstein said: 'Tell me, why do people always say it was *natural* for men to assume that the sun went round the earth rather than that the earth was rotating?' His friend said, 'Well, obviously, because it just *looks* as if the sun is going round the earth.' To which the philosopher replied, 'Well, what would it have looked like if it had looked as if the earth was rotating?'" (p. 75). As an exercise, one might imagine the various ways one could move from thinking that *obviously* it looks as if the sun is going around the earth to realizing that this is just what it would look like if the earth were rotating around the sun.

Though we need to get clear on what we could mean, the crucial conversation somehow enabled previously split-off parts of the psyche to communicate with each other. On the basis of a conversation, the structure of the psyche itself changed. How could this be?

There are three realms of inquiry that have tried to address this question: religion, philosophy, and psychoanalysis. I am not in a position to discuss religion. About philosophy, I only want to make one observation: At the origins of philosophy there seems to be an *inverse* relation between a concern with conversation and a concern with changing the structure of the psyche. Socrates is the philosophical conversationalist par excellence. If we concentrate on the early Platonic dialogues, the Socrates we meet there is very concerned with the conversation, but in each case he is trying to get his interlocutor to recognize that, unbeknownst to him, he is living with contradictory beliefs. Once the contradiction is elicited, the interlocutor is free to do anything (or nothing) in response. He may change one of his contradictory beliefs, he may change many beliefs, or he may go back to his business as though nothing had happened. Of course, any such encounter *might* have a profound effect. Perhaps a person might change profoundly in how he lived. But Socrates' only account of how that change occurred was that, through a cross-examination, he was able to expose a contradiction in that person's beliefs. The interlocutor was now in a position where he could see that at least one of his beliefs was false. And he could, if he wanted, begin an inquiry into which beliefs to expel. But the best possible outcome would be that false beliefs were rejected. There is no account about how the psyche itself might change.

By the time Plato writes *The Republic,* he is very concerned about how the psyche is shaped and about how one might change it. Plato there introduces the idea that the psyche has three parts—an appetitive part (similar to Freud's id) concerned with sex and food; a narcissistic component, called *thumos* or spirit, concerned with recognition, honor, and shame; and reason, a part of the psyche that desires to know how the world really is. There is a sophisticated account of psychic health and pathology—one that pivots around the relations of the parts of the psyche to each other, to the whole psyche, and to the world. In short, there is an account of fundamental psychic change. But a concern with Socratic conversation has fallen by the wayside.

Indeed, Book I is a dramatization of how old-fashioned Socratic conversation is useless when it comes to bringing about fundamental psychological change. For there Socrates is shown in debate with a narcissist. Thrasymachus has organized his life around *thumos,* the desire for honor and recognition. He wants to make speeches and be admired, and he has no interest in the give and take of Socratic debate. Socrates, for his part, is unwilling to make any modification to his method of cross-examination. At one point, Thrasymachus rebels: "I'm not happy with the argument you just put forward. I have some comments I would like to make on it. But if I made them, I know perfectly well you would say I was making speeches. So either let me say what I want to say, or if you want to go on asking questions, then carry on, and I'll behave as one does with an old woman telling stories. I'll say 'of course!' and nod or shake my head." He continues: "That way I'll please you, since you won't allow me to speak. What more do you want?" Astonishingly, Socrates responds: "Nothing at all. If that's what you're going to do, go ahead. I'll ask the questions."[3]

The remainder of the argument has Socrates dancing an intellectual jig around an officially compliant, but ultimately uncooperative and unpersuadable interlocutor. Perhaps, one might think, the argument wasn't really meant for Thrasymachus, it was meant to persuade the onlookers. But at the beginning of Book II, Glaucon, the deepest member of the audience, says, "Socrates, do you really want to convince us . . . or is it enough merely to seem to have convinced us?" Socrates says that he really wants to convince, and Glaucon lowers the boom: "In that case, you are not achieving your aim." From that moment on, the famous Socratic method of cross-examination is basically put into abeyance. Socrates now works *together* with Glaucon and Adeimantus, not as debating partners, but, as it were, members of the same research team, inquiring together into the nature of justice.

The rest of *The Republic* is given over to the idea that if we really want to change the structure of the psyche, we have to engage in a lot more than conversation. We have to begin with youths and shape their education as

---

3. Plato, *The Republic* I.351d-e.

well as the literature and myths they hear from the beginning, educate them gymnastically as well as ethically, make them serve in the military, study mathematics, and so on. If we simply wait until a person is an adult and then start to talk to him—well, the overwhelming suggestion is that by then it is too little, too late.[4] At the beginning of philosophy, the concern with conversation and the concern with fundamental psychic change diverge.[5]

Psychoanalysis, by contrast, is at its core a peculiar conversation among adults that aims at fundamental psychic change.[6] How does it do this? This is the question of the therapeutic action of psychoanalysis. But before we get to that question, there is a question that is even more pressing: What kind of a conversation are *we* going to have? In particular, what kind of effect is our conversa-

---

4. There is a fascinating question of what Socrates thought he was doing in his conversation with his two young-adult interlocutors, Glaucon and Adeimantus. Socrates clearly thinks there is something divine about them (II.368a), and perhaps that is why there is some point in having a conversation with them. There is also a question of what Plato thought he was doing with us, his adult readers. But these questions lie beyond the scope of this work.
5. I think one needs to wait for the sublime Kierkegaard to find a philosopher who revives the Socratic concern for conversation and tries to integrate it into a process of fundamental psychic change.
6. I do not mean to underestimate the value of child analysis, I simply want to focus on the paradigm. Also, I don't mean to imply that psychoanalysis has been clear from the beginning that this was its goal. Indeed, the early Freud (1895) was somewhat Socratic in his approach: he took himself as uncovering the "proton pseudos"— the "first falsehood"—hidden in a person's psyche.

tion going to have on therapeutic action itself? Wouldn't it be ridiculous for me—perhaps sad for you, perhaps awful for your patients—if my writing on therapeutic action had the effect of making you a worse analyst?

At first, this might seem like an overly self-conscious remark. It isn't. Let us consider, for example, the articles published in major psychoanalytic journals between 1930 and 1960. Many of them display stunning insight and depth. The overall intellectual quality is very high, and some of them are beautifully written. Yet, looking back, it seems that at the same time as these articles were being published, there emerged a generation of psychoanalysts who, overall, were too rigid, too stiff, too cut off from their patients. Did this happen in spite of all the psycho-analytic insights that were being published? Or was there something about the writing itself that facilitated the development of overly remote analysts? It seems implau-sible to assume that the writing had nothing to do with it. And it is equally implausible to assume that the prob-lem arose because everyone in that generation was grasp-ing onto falsehoods. Rather, it seems they were grasping onto truths, but in the wrong sorts of ways. For even when what was being asserted was true and informative, the manner of the writing was often too rigid. And while ana-lysts consciously learned the content of what was being said, they unconsciously internalized the form. What they learned was true; how they learned it was rigidifying.

In part this was due to a distorted conception of sci-entific rigor, which has already been much criticized, but there is a legacy that is with us still: the assumption that what matters is what we say to each other, not how we say it. Of course, scientific activity is by its nature playful as well as rigorous, often involving associations, leaps, even poetic insights. And informal communication (for example, through e-mail) makes all sorts of loops and jumps. Still, at the end of the day the aim is to test hypotheses by recognizable, repeatable, and agreed-upon methods. By the time scientists publish in journals, the aim is to publish results. Thus the paradigm form of communication is assertion: one tries to assert truths and deny falsehoods. And precisely because this form of communication is so familiar, it is easy to take it for granted. The question of how the communication occurs tends to get lost under the onslaught of assertions and denials.

Even so, it is strange that analysts have tended to ignore how they communicate with each other, since they are so sensitive to how they communicate with their analysands. Every analyst knows that in addition to the truth of what one says to an analysand, it is crucial how one says it. There is the old joke about the analyst who at the end of the first hour says, "Your case is easy: you want to kill your mother and have your father to yourself. That will be $50,000, and we don't need to meet again." The joke works because intuitively we assume what the analyst says may be true, but precisely because it is true the form of the utterance is utterly inappropriate. The comic arises out of the obvious lack of fit between form and content.

Joking aside, this is a poor interpretation because the direct form of assertion makes it impossible for the analysand to receive the content in the right sort of way. Indeed an interpretation like this, even if true—especially if true—may provoke so many defenses that the analysand can never come to learn this truth about herself. One way of not knowing is to join the analyst in making the same assertion about oneself. "You're right! I do want to kill my mother and have my father"; what one says may be true, and it may be sincerely asserted, yet it serves to insulate the analysand from making any psychic change.

Every analyst knows this. Psychoanalytic interpretation is a master art: at its finest it has the complexity and nuance of a musical performance. When it comes to interpretation, we gather up what we know about the analysand, about ourselves, about the flow of the analysis, about our language—not that we need do all this consciously. And though there is much communication between analyst and analysand that is not itself verbal, we know that how we put thought into words is crucial.

Words themselves are not going to tell us how to do this. Imagine that through a painstaking analysis, taking years, an analysand is able to recognize and work through oedipal conflicts that had been disturbing her adult life. She is now able to negotiate problems that had previously haunted her intimate life and her job, she has experienced the return of joy into her life. In a late moment of the termination phase she jokes with her analyst, "I get it now: I wanted to kill my mother and marry my father. Why didn't you just tell me at the beginning? I could have paid you $50,000 and we could have gotten it over with." Here the words are the same, and, indeed, taken as a simple assertion, they mean the same as in the previous example. But now they are uttered in a way that mocks the idea that a simple assertion could be adequate to the task. The assertion is used not only to convey a content, but also to put on display how the mere assertion of content could never convey the truth of what is being asserted. And yet by putting the inadequacy of mere assertion on display, the utterance also captures the truth of what is being uttered.

In effect, the analysand is inviting the analyst to share in a joke. They have both worked together long enough to know what is involved psychically in coming to recognize oedipal conflicts as being true about oneself. They are each in a position to grasp the wealth of psychic change that is summed up in that simple utterance. But they are also in a position to see that the assertion on its own, even though true, would have been a travesty of the truth.

Even more important, the remark now invites both analyst and analysand into an open-ended inquiry. Because the analysand's question—"Why didn't you just tell me at the beginning?"—besides being an ironic joke is also a real question. For though analyst and analysand are each in a position to see that the mere telling would have been useless, neither really understands why that is. And while the joke exposes the inadequacy of simple assertion for making certain kinds of communication, it offers no theory about how more complicated forms of communication work. How does a form of communication latch onto one's psyche? How does it make a psychic difference? This is the question of therapeutic action, and one could spend a lifetime trying to answer it.

But what kind of answer is going to work? By now it should be clear that this isn't merely a question of what the truths of therapeutic action are, it is also a question of how they are going to be communicated. Again with some notable exceptions, analysts have tended to ignore this question. How could this be? How could we be so concerned with how we communicate with our analysands, yet so thoughtless about how we communicate with each other?

There is one answer that would make sense of our behavior. If psychoanalysis were a once-and-for-all cure, then the therapeutic action would be something one could get over with. How one spoke to someone in the therapy would be delicate, but after it was over, one could revert to simple assertions. Thus analysts would have to be careful about how they communicated with their analysands, but they could speak to each other directly, in the simple mode of assertion.

One has only to state this model to see how distorted it is. The psychoanalytic process is not something that comes to an end with the termination of the actual analysis. As clinicians, as we listen to our analysands, we need to keep listening to ourselves. We need to remain sensitive to our own associations, fantasies, and inner conflicts. A psychoanalyst must always keep up her own activity of analysis as a way of continually coming back to herself as an analyst. A communication about therapeutic action ought ideally to be part of the process of developing ourselves as analysts. Certainly insofar as the formulation of the theory gets in the way of the analytic process, by encouraging a stance that is too "knowing" or too intrusive or too withdrawn, then even if the content of the theory is true, the form of communication is open to criticism.

This is an issue that is still with us. It is now widely assumed that though analysts in the past were too rigid, we can get over this problem if we concentrate instead on intersubjectivity or on object relations or two-person psychology, on the countertransference, on the interplay of transference and countertransference, and so on. No doubt this shift of concern does correct certain excesses of the past. But how will it help us come to understand the excesses of the present? The point of looking back to failures of the past is not to condescend to our predecessors, but to help us better understand how we may be distorting our own attempts to become psychoanalysts. For the real problem from the past was not so much *what* they said to each other but *how* they said it. And that problem is not going to be corrected simply by changing what we say to each other now. Clearly, there have been some changes in how we communicate with each other. There have been shifts in how all that communication and learning have been taken up by each of us in our efforts to become psychoanalysts. Nevertheless, we remain relatively unaware of how the forms of our communication influence the way we live as psychoanalysts. In this way, we are no better off than our predecessors.

We can now see the excesses of their behavior, but there is every reason to suspect that we are no better placed to spot the peculiar excesses of our time than they were placed to spot their own.

There is reason to think that being ignorant of the *how* is the disease of the current psychoanalytic profession. For it seems that the profession has lost a sense of how to absorb theory into its clinical practice. One symptom of this is a kind of institutional splitting that has occurred in the activity of psychoanalytic writing. On one side of the split, psychoanalytic theory has been taken up in humanities departments at universities throughout the United States. But the writing has become so abstract and obscure that it becomes increasingly unclear what, if anything, this has to do with psychoanalysis as it is practiced in a clinical setting. This has led clinicians on the other side of the split to think they can ignore theory altogether, or to think they can draw from it as though they were choosing from an à la carte menu. A touch of Winnicott here, a dash of Freud there, a smidgeon of Klein or Lacan—with little sense of whether these thoughts could possibly hang together. There is similarly little thought of whether they are making the right kind of application of theory to their practice. The very fact that they are in clinical practice is invoked as a trump card, as though those who live on the other side of the split couldn't really know what they are talking about. The problem is that even if you do need psychoanalytic experience to understand the theory, it is also true that if you don't understand theory you can't really understand the experience you think you are having. Theory without experience is empty; experience without theory is blind.[7]

So, how could a communication *about* therapeutic action be part *of* the therapeutic action? I have come up with an idea, and that is why I am writing. I am going to enact my own attempt to come to grips with the idea of therapeutic action, and I invite you to join me. I am going to start with a peculiar moment in my life, a moment of rupture, loss, and mourning. But actually I don't have to say much about myself to get us going.

I want to tell you about the end of a long conversation I had with the distinguished psychoanalyst Hans Loewald, but first I must briefly set the stage. I returned to the United States after having spent twelve years in Cambridge, England, studying and then teaching. Let's just say that I was trying out travel-therapy. And I did learn that whoever coined the phrase "You can't run away from your troubles" clearly hadn't traveled very much. But for some reason I felt the need to return to the geography of my sorrows, and I accepted a position teaching in the philosophy department at Yale. I knew by then that I wanted to train to be an analyst, and I applied to the Western New England Institute for Psychoanalysis, which even in England I had heard was a good institute, and one that was willing to train the occasional non-M.D. At my first meeting with my faculty advisor, he asked me whether I knew the work of Hans Loewald. I had never

---

7. Cp. Kant (1787, A51/B75).

heard of him. Loewald, it seemed, had begun his career as a philosophy graduate student in Germany under Heidegger, and my advisor thought his work might be of interest to me.

I went straight from that meeting to the Yale Co-op, bought a copy of Loewald's collected papers, went home, and read his essay, "On the Therapeutic Action of Psychoanalysis" (1960). I think of that as my first act as an analyst-in-training. Even though my understanding of analysis was rudimentary, I knew at once that this essay was a classic. Positive transference you will say. To be sure. And yet every time I have gone back to that essay over the subsequent two decades, I have always felt it leap out to meet me. No matter what stage of life I am in, that essay reaffirms itself as a classic.

I made an appointment to meet with Loewald. Although I was myself a professor of philosophy, I asked Loewald if I could hire him as my tutor. I would pay him his regular hourly fee to meet with him once a week to talk about his ideas. He agreed, and so began a weekly conversation that stretched out six or seven years, much of it about the therapeutic action of psychoanalysis. I tell you this in order to tell you about the last moment of that conversation. By now he was in a nursing home, he wasn't charging me any more, and he was taken up in various ways with the unpleasant business of being in decline. A few days before he died, Hans expressed the hope that there would never be any Loewaldians. These were not his last words, but they were his last words to me. What might he have meant?

I didn't ask. In a way this was strange, because for years our conversation had largely consisted in me asking him what he meant. Why the sudden reticence on my part? In part, I thought I understood: names, by their nature, tend to deaden thought. People call themselves (or others) Freudians, or Lacanians, or Kleinians, or object relations theorists or intersubjectivists or relational theorists or . . . and precisely by having a name they no longer have to think about what they mean by it. (At a cocktail party, should it emerge I am trained as a psychoanalyst, people will ask whether I am a "strict Freudian," and I have to remind myself that they may not know what they mean by their own question. Usually the question means something like: Am I dogmatic, cold, and rigidly clinging to outdated ideas? Difficult to answer that question with a ringing affirmative! Ironically, the question of how my thoughts might actually relate to Freud's has not even been asked, and it is the very word "Freudian" that disguises the fact that we are not really talking about much of anything.) The last thing Hans would have wanted was to have his thinking killed off by a bunch of people who called themselves Loewaldians.

I also knew that Loewald was a humble man. He spent his days seeing patients, but evenings and weekends were spent in the company not only of his family but of Freud and Heidegger and Kierkegaard. He saw himself as a Freudian—a creative explicator of Freud—and thus it would make no sense to think of himself as founding a line of thought that deserved its own name.

But there is another reason I didn't ask. We both knew that he was dying, and we both knew that we knew. Loewald wasn't expressing an abstract wish, this was a deathbed wish, expressed directly to me. He was trying to let me know that there were certain paths of mourning that, in his opinion, would be inappropriate. Perhaps I was shy in the face of a dying man, but I also felt that Hans was leaving it to me to figure out what he meant. Or to figure out what I might mean. Though it was his wish, the task of living with it was now mine—and neither he nor anyone else could figure out *on my behalf* how to live with that wish.

As I said, Hans died, and for about a decade I had a stable sense of how to live with his wish. I did write an article about his work, I wrote an introduction to a collection of his writings, but I was careful to stress that Loewald's work represented a deep interpretation of Freud. I abjured overstatement, and I tried to get on with my own reading of Freud, which I thought was a good way to honor the memory of Hans Loewald.

There things rested until recently when, in reading a passage from Kierkegaard, my previous understanding was shattered by laughter. *From* Kierkegaard, but not *by* Kierkegaard: *The Concluding Unscientific Postscript* is written under the pseudonym of Johannes Climacus. But unlike an ordinary pseudonym, Climacus is the name of an author who Kierkegaard himself created. It is Climacus who then went on to write this book. Kierkegaard created various authors, and in "A First and Last Declaration" he says, "My wish, my prayer, is that if it might occur to anyone to quote a particular saying from the books, he would do me the favor to cite the name of the respective pseudonymous author."[8] Is this Kierkegaard's way of saying he hopes there will never be any Kierkegaardians? Certainly, it is his way of saying that he doesn't want anyone to think of herself as a Kierkegaardian simply by taking up something a pseudonym has written. So let us stick with Climacus.

Climacus is concerned with the form that certain communications must take. He considers the case of a religious person who comes to think he should have no disciples:

> Suppose thus, that it happened to be the view of life of a religiously existing subject, that no man ought to have any disciple, that having disciples is an act of treason to God and man; suppose he also happened to be a little stupid (for if something more than honesty is required to make one's way through the world, it is always necessary to be stupid in order to have real success, and in order to be thoroughly understood by the many), and asserted this principle directly, with pathos and unction: what would happen? Why then he would be understood; and he would soon have applications from at least ten candidates, offering to preach this doctrine, in return merely for a free shave once a week. That is to say, he would in further confirmation of his doctrine have experienced

8. Soren Kierkegaard, "A First and Last Declaration," in Kierkegaard. (1846, p. 552).

the peculiar good fortune of obtaining disciples to accept
and disseminate this doctrine of not having any disciples.[9]

Strictly speaking, this religious savant does not contradict himself. For example, he does not assert, say, that
God exists and then go on to contradict himself by saying that He also does not exist. There need be no incon-
sistency in what he *says*. Rather, if there is a problem here
it lies in an irresolvable tension between *what* he says and
how he says it. More generally, there is a tension between
what he says, no matter how sincerely, and how he lives.
Let us assume that he is sincere in wanting no disciples;
his communication is virtually guaranteed to attract disciples who will preach that there should be no disciples.

It dawned on me that the task of *not* being a
Loewaldian was unproblematic. All I had to do was refrain from becoming a Loewaldian, in some tired sense
of those words. I assumed, that is, that all I had to do was
refrain from preaching a Loewaldian gospel, refrain from
giving talks in which I insisted that Loewald represented
a new school of thought, refrain from talking about a
Loewaldian approach—and that was about it.

It dawned on me that the task of *not* being a
Loewaldian was more difficult than I had supposed. For
suppose a group of intelligent and well-meaning psychoanalytic thinkers—themselves fascinated by Loewald's

---

9. Ibid., p. 70. I am indebted to my colleague James Conant and to
the members of a seminar we jointly taught on *The Concluding Unscientific Postscript* for an understanding of this passage.

thought—began to write about the Loewaldian approach, began, indeed, to call themselves Loewaldians. I would recognize that something had gone wrong in the communication between Loewald and his readers, but what could I do about it? Certainly, I couldn't simply *say*, "Loewald wanted no disciples" or "Loewald hoped that there wouldn't be any Loewaldians." On its own, such a declaration would just encourage its own perverse form of discipleship. We, the "knowing group," could go around, perhaps with an esoteric wink, saying that to truly understand Loewald is to understand that there should be no Loewaldians. And now we would be teaching a new kind of discipleship for the man who wants no disciples.

Maybe this doesn't strike you as funny, but for me it was hilarious. Suddenly I realized that to not be a Loewaldian, it wasn't enough simply to refrain from becoming a Loewaldian, whatever that means; one had to not be a Loewaldian in *the right sort of way!* But what way was that? And I then realized that the world has enough how-to books; but we are sorely lacking a *how-not-to* book. Is there a way I could teach how *not* to be a disciple that would get it right?

Now in Climacus' story, the religious figure is somewhat insightful, but he also happens to be "a little bit stupid": he asserts his principle "directly, with pathos and unction." Does that mean that Hans was being "a little bit stupid" when he spoke so directly to me? But maybe he wasn't speaking to me directly. What would that mean? Well, if he were speaking to me directly, I suppose he would be thinking that there was some definite body of doctrine that composed his views. To assert that doctrine on the basis of Loewald's teachings would be what it was to be a Loewaldian. So, if Hans had been speaking directly, he would have been expressing the hope that there would never be any such people. Hans could not have meant that. So, what if he were speaking to me indirectly? He would then be inviting me to see that the reason he hoped there would be no Loewaldians is because there couldn't possibly be any. There was no body of doctrine with which Loewald took to be his own. So there was nothing to take up, nothing to assert on his behalf. And if anyone took up the position of Loewaldian, it would have to be in the context of a massive misunderstanding of what one could possibly be. The problem wouldn't be so much that *what* he was saying was false, but that *how* he was living was confused.

If one could sort out *that* confusion, it would be part of therapeutic action. And, indeed, I can now recognize Hans's last words to me as a gift. For if Hans really were concerned that there should be no Loewaldians, it showed remarkable trust in me that he should say so. He trusted me to understand him. Or he trusted me to live in such a way that I could, over time, come to understand him. And there is every reason to think that he was genuinely concerned. This wasn't just coy or false modesty or precious paradox. Hans had devoted his life to a certain kind of questioning—of himself and others—a kind of questioning that was itself a form of life. It was his life. Its point was not to come to an end in a body of doctrine, a fixed set of answers. Indeed, coming to such a resting place would itself be a failure, a betrayal of that form of life. If I had come away from our conversation thinking, "The answer is not to be a Loewaldian," that would have been as much a betrayal, and as much of a confusion, as thinking, "The answer is to be a Loewaldian." For the essential problem would be neither with being or not being a Loewaldian, but with thinking there was an answer.

The religious leader in Climacus' example looks ridiculous, so it is important to remember he is taking a terrible risk. It is his view of life that "having disciples is an act of treason to God and man." Thus if he ends up having disciples, it is a disaster *for him.* Climacus draws him with the broad strokes of caricature; he tells us only that he asserts his thesis directly, "with pathos and unction," and the reader is left to fill in the picture. I imagine him decked out in lace and a flowing black robe, high up on a pulpit, declaiming in a thunderous voice, "Thou shalt have no disciples!" No sooner has he spoken than several people jump up from the back pews, "Quick, let's spread our leader's teaching!" But I can imagine a less grotesque figure who uttered words that were similar to the words Hans Loewald used with me. Perhaps he once said, "I hope I have no disciples for this reason: a religious person should have no disciples." He might remain "a little bit stupid," but then his stupidity would consist less in what he said than in how he said it and in *whom he said it to.* He may be confused, but in his eyes treason before God is at stake; his own eternal fate hangs on how those who listen to him proceed. Perhaps that is why he is so ludicrous; considering how much seems to be at stake for him, he has given so little thought to how to live and how to communicate.

Loewald spent his life thinking about how to live and how to communicate, and his life embodied that thought. I have certainly come to recognize that understanding him does not mean grasping a doctrine that, once I have learned it, I can pass on to others. But, then, what could it mean to understand him? It's no good just *saying* that the psychoanalytic life is a life of inquiry, questioning, interpretation, and activity, and not a life-asserting doctrine. That is just one more assertion of doctrine. Somehow the understanding must be embodied in the activity of communicating. This is an instance of a more general question: What would it be to write psychoanalytically about psychoanalysis?

This may seem to you like sailing very close to the wind, but an answer that pleases me is to write an essay on the central concepts of psychoanalysis—concepts that were taken up earlier by Freud and then again by Loewald in his classic essay, "On the Therapeutic Action of Psychoanalysis." But isn't this to violate Loewald's own wish? Isn't this to encourage people to become Loewaldians? Just the opposite, I think. I should like to do a reading of Loewald that brings out the activity of psychoanalytic thinking, that reveals in a liberating way that there is nothing to be Loewaldian about. I should like to participate in a discussion of therapeutic action that itself might be continuous with the process of therapeutic action. The essay as a whole would be an expression of how not to be a Loewaldian in the right sort of way.

This hardly seems like a best-seller-in-the-making. Thank goodness! As you can probably tell by now, the last thing I need is disciples—even worse, to be caught writing in a way the promotes the founding of the School of Loewald. To a significant extent, I am writing this book for myself: to go through a kind of conceptual therapy whereby I hope to deepen myself as an analyst. But I am also reaching out to those readers who might find going through a similar process enlivening for them. If you can draw this book into your own living attempts to become an analyst of the psyche, marvelous! I'd love this book to be a best-seller for a few. Not because the doctrine is esoteric: there are no secrets here.[10] But because the work is aimed to make a difference for those who are already embarked on their own paths of therapeutic action.

---

10. Actually, let me quickly mention the only morsel that might be considered esoteric. This is for the reader who enjoys somewhat arcane details. I am inspired to write this essay by Climacus' account of the conversation between Lessing and Jacobi. Climacus puts before us a Jacobi who, with all his earnest enthusiasm, simply cannot begin to understand his ironic "teacher" Lessing. Lessing is someone who in his style and form of communication did everything in his power to defeat having disciples, and yet he attracts a Jacobi who thoroughly misunderstands him. Even worse, almost everything that remains in the popular understanding of what Kierkegaard meant by the need to take a leap derives from this account of Jacobi. So, the popular understanding of Kierkegaard arises from a book by Climacus (one of his authors who Kierkegaard declares is not him), and, indeed, from the context of a dramatization of how one thinker can thoroughly misunderstand another. (See "Theses Possibly or Actually Attributable to Lessing," in Kierkegaard 1846, book II, part I, chapter 2.) And I thought to myself: can I do a better job with Loewald than Jacobi did with Lessing?

2

Subjectivity, Objectivity, and Irony

There is a crucial ambiguity in the term *therapeutic action*. On the one hand, it refers to the process, *whatever it is*, by which the patient gets better. In this sense, it is like an *x* in algebra: in trying to figure out how psychoanalysis works, we are in effect trying to solve for the equation, *therapeutic action* = *x*. On the other hand, it also describes all of our actions insofar as we are facilitating a therapeutic process. As analysts, our acts—listening, being there, questions, associations, interpretations—ought to be therapeutic acts. But what grounds our confidence that our acts are therapeutic acts? Insofar as the therapeutic action of psychoanalysis remains an enigmatic *x*, how do we know that our acts are facilitating it?

This is not simply a question about psychoanalysis, it is a question about our own identity. For *psychoanalyst* is not simply a term like *newspaper reader* or *airline passenger*, which describe things we do, even things we do often or are committed to. *Psychoanalyst* describes who we are. There are three related features of being a psychoanalyst that command our attention. First, as psychoanalysts, we are constantly in the process of shaping ourselves as psychoanalysts. As we listen to our analysands, we are also listening to ourselves. We wonder about what conflicts are being stirred up in our analysands, and we also wonder about what conflicts are being stirred up in ourselves. We strive to shape ourselves into people who can listen well and who can intervene in ways that are genuinely helpful to our analysands. This is a process of becoming a certain kind of a person.

Second, the process is unending. No matter how experienced we are as psychoanalysts, there is always the question, How does this next thought, this next act, this next intervention contribute to the therapeutic action? We are regularly brought up short by our analysands, surprised by the flow of our own emotional lives. Being a psychoanalyst is in part a never-ending task of bringing oneself back to the activity of being a psychoanalyst. It is not a rote activity, so that once you've done it, there's really no problem involved in doing it again. To put it paradoxically: to *be* an analyst one must ever be in the process of *becoming* an analyst. For anyone for whom the process of becoming is over, he or she has ceased to be an analyst. In that sense, being an analyst is a constant process of re-creative repetition. It is the unending project of remembering—as one re-creates—what it is to be an analyst.[1]

Third, this process of continually coming back to ourselves as psychoanalysts is itself part of the therapeutic action, in both of the above senses. As psychoanalysts, we began our training with our own analysis. We hope that the therapeutic action of that analysis enabled us eventually to get up from the couch and continue on as analysts. For therapeutic action does not describe a process, like getting a tattoo, which has a fixed end point. Once you've gotten a tattoo, you've got a tattoo; indeed, once you've had an analysis, you've had an analysis, but therapeutic action goes on and on. Analysis has a termination, therapeutic action does not. Ideally, one continues one's own process of therapeutic action as a lifetime project. As an analyst, this process is lived out in the myriad activities of facilitating therapeutic action in others.

Thus a book about therapeutic action ought ideally to be an occasion for therapeutic action itself. It ought to be an occasion for analysts to continue on with their

---

1. A colleague of mine told me this anecdote: Loewald, then a distinguished analyst in his 70s, had fallen ill and taken some time off, but was now on the mend. He bumped into my friend, who was at the time a young analyst, at the psychoanalytic institute. Loewald asked this young analyst to keep him in mind for referrals. My friend was surprised that such a distinguished analyst would actually be looking for patients, but before he could finish having that thought, Loewald said, "You know, I'd like to keep my hand in. I think I'm beginning to get the hang of it."

own processes of therapeutic action. But how can a book facilitate this? This is not an easy question to answer, for there is a peculiar problem that haunts all attempts at theoretical communication. The terms with which we communicate, no matter what they are—"unconscious" or "ego" or "intersubjectivity" or "object relations" or "bad breast" or "play of signifiers"—tend to lose their vibrancy as they are passed along in the community. This is the entropy of thought: whatever life the concepts might have had when they are first being applied in vivid psychoanalytic contexts tends to get drained out of them, and they get turned more and more into slogans. Eventually, the terms get used in place of thinking rather than as an expression of it. The ultimate absurdity is a dead paper on therapeutic action.

The entropy of thought is not a problem that can be completely avoided. It is endemic to thinking itself. Even the phrase "entropy of thought" can become a cliché. So, too, can warnings to avoid it. So, the task for us is to bring our concepts to life.

It is crucial that we try, for psychoanalysis is essentially committed to its own transparency. This does not mean that analysands should learn psychoanalytic theory. Indeed, our patients often get interested in theory as a defense against the psychoanalytic process. Still, there should be no *essential* secrets. By contrast, for a magic trick to work, it is essential that the audience not see the sleights of hand by which the effect is produced. There are cultures in which a voodoo curse can have powerful effects on the recipient. But it is crucial to the "thera-

peutic action" of voodoo that the recipient not understand how voodoo really works. And while it might just
be possible for there to be a cynical witch doctor—a pigmy
Wizard of Oz—still it is much easier for him to carry out
his curse if he too remains confused about what he is
doing. One might thus say that it is essential to the practice of voodoo that the voodoo theory of voodoo mislead the participants. The participants have to think that
the curse works *by* voodoo—and though the curse may
indeed work, that is not how it is happening.

   Psychoanalysis stands to voodoo, to hypnosis, and
to other forms of suggestion as philosophy stands to sophistry. It is a constitutive contrast. We may spend our lives
trying to figure out what philosophy is, but one of our
permanent touchstones is that it is not sophistry. Indeed,
as soon as we can identify a form of argument as so-
phistical, we are in a position to refine our sense of what
philosophy is by rejecting that kind of argument from
the repertoire. Indeed, figuring out the difference between philosophy and sophistry is itself part of the therapeutic action of philosophy. So, too, when we can identify
a certain form of human interaction as "suggestion," we
are in a position to reject it as part of psychoanalytic technique. And this attempt to root out suggestion will be a
lifelong commitment because, like voodoo, its myriad
forms will tend to hide the fact that they are forms of
suggestion.

   So the challenge is to make psychoanalysis transpar-
ent in a psychoanalytically vibrant way. In this spirit, we
might go back to Loewald's (1960) essay in the way that

an analysand goes back to an earlier stage of her life. The point of going back to that moment is not simply so that we should understand it better, it is as a way of coming to understand ourselves better—as a way of taking up our past and going on from here. "On the Therapeutic Action of Psychoanalysis" was first published in the *International Journal of Psycho-Analysis* in 1960. That means that it was composed in the late 1950s, and that the author took himself to be addressing an audience mainly of medical doctors who had further trained as psychoanalysts. This is who we were.

At first, it may seem absurd to treat this as *our* past. After all, many of us analysts today never trained as medical doctors. And even those of us who have trained no longer identify with the ego ideals of the medical profession circa 1950. Why go back to that dead past? Yet, in the treatment of individuals we regularly find that a supposedly dead past continues to exert an uncanny influence. We see pathologies get transmitted from generation to generation without anyone in the family understanding what is happening. Might not something similar be happening at the professional level? Indeed, from a psychoanalytic point of view, the very fact that this past seems dead is all the more reason to go back to it. Perhaps in the very experience of its seeming dead we will come to recognize a current resistance on our part—perhaps a resistance to recognizing who we are.

So, for example, Loewald begins with fundamental claims that analysts made about themselves—namely, that they were neutral and objective. And there is certainly the temptation to think, For goodness sakes, what does this have to do with us?! We analysts know that we are subjective and emotionally engaged with our analysands. But what is it we really know? *Objective* and *subjective* are a contrasting pair, but in different contexts they can be used to make various contrasts. If we don't really understand what, in a given context, is meant by *objective*, then it is not going to be of help simply to flip over to the other member of the pair, *subjective*. Whatever unclarity there is about the first member of the pair will be preserved as we flip over to the second. The real challenge that faces us is not to figure out which concept, *objective* or *subjective*, applies to us; it is to figure out what either concept could possibly mean. It is a feature of the concept of objectivity that it is notoriously difficult to pin down. Yet analysts in the 1950s invoked it to describe themselves. Thus if there are confusions in this concept it must go to the heart of their self-understanding. And it is no help for us to say, "That's not our problem, we're all intersubjectivists now." The point of our inquiry is not simply to grasp how an earlier generation got confused about objectivity; it is to help us gain insight into how we might be confused in similar ways about intersubjectivity, about object relations, about whatever the current concepts are with which we try to understand ourselves.

What are the concepts of subjectivity and objectivity that are appropriate to us as psychoanalysts? It seems to me that we should begin by returning to a primordial meaning of subjectivity. Let us say that a concept is subjective if it names a certain kind of a subject—to be de-

scribed as follows. *Lover* is a subjective concept in the
sense that someone who loves is constantly in the process of shaping herself into a person who loves. She is
constantly in the process of becoming a certain kind of a
subject. This is an unending project. A person can dedicate her life to better understanding—and better living
out—what it is to love others. There is no end to the
ever-deepening complexity—or simplicity—of the
project. Should one get to an end, all this can mean is
that one gets stuck. Or, worse, that one ceases to love.
Furthermore, the lover essentially uses the concept of
love in her never-ending project of becoming/being a
lover. It is in continually asking the question, "What is it
to love (this person, this idea)?" that the lover continues
to shape herself as a lover.

We have already seen that *psychoanalyst* is a subjective concept in this sense. The psychoanalyst constitutes
herself as a certain kind of subject by repeatedly and cre-
atively bringing herself back to the project of becoming/
being a psychoanalyst. Thus we have isolated a use of
subjectivity that stresses the fact that the psychoanalyst is
a certain kind of subject. There are other meanings of
subjectivity to which we, as psychoanalysts, avail ourselves,
but this one, I suggest, should be preeminent.

Having done this conceptual work, we are now in a
position to formulate a *subjective use of objectivity*. That is,
in forming ourselves as psychoanalysts, what conception
of objectivity is needed for our task? Is there a conception of objectivity that would be appropriate in our never-
ending project of calling ourselves back to the task of

being psychoanalysts? What are the real needs in the context of which the concepts of objectivity and neutrality might legitimately help us to understand ourselves?

First, we invoke these concepts as ideals, to help us in our own emotional self-regulation. We try to keep the analytic situation free "from being contaminated by the analyst's own emotional intrusions."[2] Again there is the facile objection that nowadays we recognize that the analyst must of course bring her emotional life into the analytic situation. Indeed, we shouldn't pretend to analysands that we are unfeeling creatures. It helps them to know who we are, emotionally speaking. The response to this objection is not so much that it is wrong; indeed, in some sense it is true. But it misses a crucial point. What we are concerned with are emotional *intrusions* that by their very nature disrupt the analytic process. To take an exaggerated example, should the analyst start crying because the analysand is, after all, not going to become a lawyer as his mother wanted? No one would think this was a legitimate example of the analyst's letting the analysand know how she feels. This is a caricature, but it reminds us that there are all sorts of emotional intrusions, and it is constitutive of our life as analysts that we try to refrain from them. When we get to less extreme examples, there is not going to be any fixed or clear-cut answer as to what parts of our lives as human beings constitute an emotional intrusion. That's why working out

---

2. Loewald (1960) in Loewald (2000, p. 223).

what constitutes an emotional intrusion is itself a lifetime project that is never finished. Or rather, when we finish with that project, we cease to be analysts. The concepts of neutrality and objectivity are ideals that we use to bring ourselves back to that lifetime project of trying to figure out how to live as analysts.

Second, the analyst must maintain herself in such a way that she can both receive the analysand's transference projections and then reflect them back to the analysand in verbal communications that the analysand can himself recognize. To continue with the caricatured example, if the analysand says, "You're acting just like my mother!" there is no way he could come to recognize this as a transference, even if it was, for whatever is happening with him psychically, the analyst *is* acting just like his mother. Precisely because what the analysand is saying is true, there is no room for him to recognize how it might be true and how it might be false. Again, the analyst invokes concepts like objectivity and neutrality in order to help her maintain herself in a position in which she can continue to reflect the analysand's conscious and unconscious mental processes.

In short, the concept of objectivity has a potentially important role to play within the context of the analyst's own attempts to sustain herself as an analyst. Anyone who practices psychoanalysis knows that it is an unending task. We are constantly being brought up short by our analysands, constantly being surprised by the flow of our own emotional lives. Being a psychoanalyst is in part a never-ending task of bringing oneself back to the activity of being a psychoanalyst.

As Loewald puts it, "Objectivity and neutrality need to be understood more clearly as to their meaning in a therapeutic setting."[3] The danger—in terms of self-misunderstanding—would be to think that the concept of objectivity comes with a fixed and determinate meaning, independent of the context in which it is deployed. We then set ourselves up for the misconception that the only use of objectivity is, as it were, an objective use of objectivity. There are many facts that need only be asserted, for example, that water is composed of H_2O. Or, if we want to talk about humans, that metabolism occurs according to the Kreb's cycle, or that transmission of neuronal firing across a synapse can be inhibited. At least, we think they are facts, and given that, we feel free simply to assert them. Even though these claims are true or false about humans, they play no particular role in a person's attempts to build him- or herself up into a subject.[4]

There is no particular problem either with the subjective use or the objective use of objectivity. Problems

---

3. Loewald (1960), op. cit., p. 223.
4. Indeed, as we shall see, this is a bit of an exaggeration, for a person may be trying to build herself up into a knower and communicator of truths. The point though is that there are certain truths that are simply true, and as such can simply be asserted. They need play no particular role in the subject forming herself as a subject.

arise when we confuse the two, and, in effect, this is what
Loewald thinks we have done in our efforts to understand the psychoanalytic situation. The annotations
within square brackets are my own indications of how I
think this passage should be read:

> The objectivity of the analyst in regard to the patient's
> transference distortions, his neutrality in this [subjec-
> tive] sense, should not be confused with the "neutral"
> attitude of the pure scientist towards his subject of study.
> Nevertheless, the relationship between a scientific ob-
> server and his subject of study has been taken as the model
> for the analytic relationship, with the following deviation:
> the subject, under the specific conditions of the analytic
> experiment, directs his activities towards the observer, and
> the observer communicates his findings directly to the
> subject with the goal of modifying the findings. *These de-*
> *viations from the model, however, change the whole structure of*
> *the relationship to the extent that the model is not representative*
> *and useful but, indeed misleading. . . .*
>   While the relationship between analyst and patient
> does not possess the structure, scientist-scientific sub-
> ject, and is not characterized by neutrality in that sense
> on the part of the analyst, the analyst may become [sub-
> jectively] a scientific observer to the extent to which he
> is able [subjectively] to observe the patient and himself
> in interaction. The interaction itself, however, cannot
> be adequately represented by the model of [objective]
> scientific neutrality. It is [objectively] unscientific, based
> on faulty observation, to use this model. . . . What I am

attempting to do is to disentangle the justified and necessary requirement of [subjective] objectivity and neutrality from a model of [objective] neutrality which has its origin in propositions which I believe to be untenable.[5]

The problem then is that the conception of objectivity within psychoanalysis is a confused melange. It starts from a legitimate need for some conception of objectivity—one that is appropriate for the distinctive activity of psychoanalysis—but then assumes that there is only one fixed conception of objectivity, that which is bequeathed to us by the (physical) sciences of the early twentieth century. And the confusion is only compounded if, seeing how inappropriate this conception of objectivity is for psychoanalysis, we simply throw out the concept of objectivity altogether. "We're all intersubjectivists now!" In the name of change, we are unconsciously remaining the same: for both sides of this debate share the assumption that there is one fixed conception of objectivity—one side deeming it appropriate, the other inappropriate. And by simply throwing out the concept of objectivity, we mislead ourselves about our own needs. Rather than choose between this either/or, a conceptual working-through is in order.

One might begin by reflecting on the fact that *scientist* is itself a subjective category. That is, a scientist should be perpetually asking herself whether she is shaping herself to pursue her inquiries in the right sorts of ways. The

---

5. Loewald (1960), op. cit., pp. 226–227.

question of whether I am inquiring into this or that realm in ways that are appropriate for yielding knowledge is not one that should go away. Indeed, I constitute myself as a scientist by keeping myself open to changing how I investigate the realm that matters to me, in light of better understandings of what it would be to yield knowledge in that realm. It is essential to being a scientist that I ever be engaged with the question of how to live as a scientist. What counts as scientific is the activity of a scientist who behaves appropriately as such.

Even in the sciences the concept of objectivity is essentially subjective; as I shape myself as a scientist, I must ask, What are the norms of inquiry, discovery, and communication that make my research objective? Here, it seems to me, we need to return to a primordial conception of objectivity: the idea that we are relating to objects with sufficient respect for their being objects. That is, we are relating objectively to objects when we recognize that they are to a certain extent self-standing, that they have certain claims to stand out from the environment in which they are located, certain claims to independence, certain claims to reality. We also recognize that objects have by their natures many facets and dimensions.[6] Ironically, we shape ourselves into a certain kind of subject, a scientist, when we discipline ourselves into relating objectively to objects. This becomes less paradoxical-seeming when we reflect on the

---

6. As Kant (1787) memorably put it, "An object is that in the concept of which the manifold of a given intuition is united" (p. B137).

fact that relating objectively to objects is, to a significant extent, a matter of respect.

Obviously, the precise nature of that respect will shift
from science to science. A marine biologist will comport
herself differently toward an amoeba than an astronomer does toward a distant galaxy than a topologist does
toward string. But in each case the scientist will be showing a respect toward the self-standingness of the object of
inquiry that is itself appropriate to that area of inquiry. In
general, it will remain a never-ending question of which
modes of inquiry are appropriate. So, for example, an astronomer of today will observe black holes in ways that
would be virtually unrecognizable to an astronomer of the
nineteenth century. Not only have the objects of study
changed, what counts as an observation, as a confirmation or disconfirmation, has been utterly transformed. But
what remains constant through this transformation is the
attempt to form a mode of inquiry that respects the objectivity of this particular kind of object.

When it comes to psychoanalysis we are dealing with
human beings—and human beings are indeed a peculiar kind of object. In particular, they are objects that are
capable of becoming (being) subjects. And though we
will be interacting with them—indeed, as psychoanalysts
we shall facilitate certain kinds of change—we still need
a conception of humans that respects them as (relatively
and appropriately) self-standing, as having their own
points of view, their own claims for independence, their
own possession of aspects that may elude our notice or
understanding. In psychoanalysis in particular we need

to respect the reality of another person's unconscious; we need to respect the reality of their psychic reality. And precisely because a person's psychic reality is not immediately available to their conscious awareness, we need to formulate appropriate methods for eliciting it. All of this should hold true no matter what particular school of psychoanalysis one adheres to. If I am concentrating on the intersubjective field, for example, or on the flow of transference and countertransference emotions, I still need to track the contributions we each are making to that field. In short, if I am going to fashion myself into a psychoanalyst, I need a conception of objectivity that is appropriate to my being a psychoanalyst. This is a subjective use of objectivity. In its broadest and deepest sense, this is an ethical notion: not in the sense that it has to do particularly with morality, but in the sense that it is essentially concerned with how to live. And it is essentially a respectful form of living.

The analytic process, according to Loewald, facilitates the new discovery of objects:

> I say new discovery of objects, and not discovery of new objects, because the essence of such new object-relationships is the opportunity they offer for rediscovery of the early paths of the development of object-relations, leading to a new way of relating to objects as well as of being and relating to oneself. This new discovery of oneself and of objects, this reorganization of ego and objects, is made possible by the encounter with a "new object" that has to possess certain qualifications in order

to promote the process. Such a new object-relationship for which the analyst holds himself available to the patient and to which the patient has to hold on throughout the analysis is one meaning of the term *positive transference.*[7]

We began with a confused idea of objectivity, but instead of simply rejecting it, we worked our way to a more primordial meaning which lies at the heart of the analytic process. Now we have a conception of objectivity such that not only does the analyst need to maintain objectivity, but it is an aspiration of the analysis that the analysand takes on a more objective point of view. This is the new discovery of objects (as opposed to the discovery of new objects). The analyst facilitates a process (the nature of which needs to be discussed) by which the analysand slowly comes to recognize that what he had taken to be the world as it really is, is in fact the imposition of a distorting point of view. The analysand has been living with a skewed view of himself and others, and all along he has assumed that he has been the passive recipient of the world as it really is. What he had taken to be objective is in fact subjective.

The analytic process allows the analysand to relate to objects in new sorts of ways—to relate to them as distinct persons, having their own points of view—that is, to relate to them objectively. This opens up new ways of relating to others, but it also opens up new ways of relating to oneself: for now one is able to live with others as

7. Loewald (1960), op. cit., p. 225.

the distinct and real people they are. Becoming objective in this sense opens up the possibility for true human intimacy. For previously one was not genuinely relating to another—or rather, insofar as one did relate to others, it was through the confusing fog of one's own wishes, hopes, and disappointments, which were regularly experienced as being in the other.

At the beginning of an analysis, what the analysand lacks is a subjective use for the concept of objectivity. He takes the world, including the social world, as given. It is as though he were a passive recipient of reality—at least, that is how it seems to him. By now it is familiar that the beginning analysand is largely unaware of his own activity, unaware of his projections onto the world, and unaware of his distortions of it. But it remains unfamiliar that this lack of awareness is facilitated by a confusion of his own relation to objectivity. He lacks the ability to ask the following question in a genuine or full way: "Given that I wish to become/be a certain kind of a subject—a lover, a creative person, a friend, a parent, a son or daughter, a true professional, etc.—what is the correct view of the social world, what is the correct view of my inner world, that I can use to deepen myself as the subject I wish to become/be?" Lacking the ability to ask this question, ideas of objectivity tend to get used as a defense.

Let me give an example.

A patient of mine inhabited a disappointing world. Although she was quite successful at work, had friends, and so on, there was no success in the social world that would not be interpreted by her under an aura of disappointment. If she got a raise at work, it was because the boss was shamed into it—he really wanted to give someone else in the office a raise, but he felt he had to give her one to appear fair. If she was invited out for a date, the person had already tried to go out with others and had failed. If someone congratulated her on some accomplishment, they were just being polite. And so on. From a distance it is clear to us, as it was not clear to her, how active she was in understanding her world in ways that were bound to disappoint. And, of course, much of the analysis was spent working through these repetitive attempts at disappointment.

But if we ask ourselves, What did this working-through consist in?, it is not enough to say that it consisted in helping her to see how active she was in creating her own disappointments. For that transition itself consisted in a shift in her own conception of objectivity. That is, it was easier for her to experience the world as itself disappointing if she experienced the nature of the world as utterly independent of her. It was as though disappointment were written into the stars. Obviously, she did not have an explicit concept of objectivity—she was not about to make a speech about what objectivity meant for her—but her understanding of objectivity was implicit in the ways she inhabited and understood her world.

It seems to me that developing a subjective sense of objectivity was crucial to the analysis. For if one lives with a confused but overall objective sense of objectivity, it is as though the human world is like the stars—it is just the way it is. But as one develops a concern for oneself as a subject—concern for oneself as someone who sincerely wants to ask the question of how she should live—then the question of objectivity becomes a question of understanding the world aright, in terms of one's own decisions of how to live within it. That shift to a subjective conception of objectivity occurs when one is able to ask oneself, "Am I sure I understand the boss correctly when he gave me a raise?" In the confused sense of objectivity, the sense of the way the world is is meant to preclude any further questions about it. That's the way the world is, and that's that. In the subjective sense of objectivity, by contrast, there is always a further question about whether I have understood myself and others accurately. For now we raise the question of objectivity within the context of our own concerned engagement in the world, and in a context where it clearly matters to be getting things right. When one is concerned with the human realm, that is, the realm of hopes and fears and desires and wishes and projects and designs, the objective use of objectivity closes down questions, and the subjective use of objectivity opens them up.

Once we can see the analysand as moving from an objective to a subjective use of objectivity, we can see that the analyst is herself engaged in essentially the same process as the analysand. Indeed, they are moving in tandem. For the analyst is ever renewing herself in her efforts to understand herself, her patients, and her friends and loved ones, clearly and well. This activity is the repetitive re-creation of herself as an analyst. This essentially involves subjective use of the concept of objectivity. As Loewald puts it:

> It also needs to be said that the love of truth is no less a passion because it desires truth rather than some less elevated end. In our field, the love of truth cannot be isolated from the passion for truth to ourselves and truth in human relationships. In other fields, too, the scientist is filled with love for his object precisely in his most creative and "dispassionate" moments. Scientific detachment in its genuine form, far from excluding love is based on it. In our work it can be truly said that in our best moments of dispassionate and objective analyzing we love our object, the patient, more than at any other time and are compassionate with his whole being. In our field scientific spirit and care for the object certainly are not opposites; they flow from the same source.[8]

At first, it might seem ridiculous that in our most dispassionate and objective moments we manifest our greatest love. But now that we have worked through the concepts of subjectivity and objectivity, we are able to recognize the possibility of a certain kind of passion in our dispassion. It was the possibility for this peculiar kind of passion that was all but missing before the therapy began.

---

8. "Analytic Theory and the Analytic Process," in Loewald (2000), op. cit., p. 297.

Remember the analysts of the 1950s who are now criticized for being too dispassionate, too cold, and too unloving? Even if this is a caricature, let us stick with the grain of truth within it. Given the confused conception of objectivity they were working with, there was no room for them to understand how a dispassionate stance can be passionate and loving. The very idea of objectivity that they lived with served to preclude the idea of objectivity as itself an expression of love. Loewald's strategy was not to reject objectivity, but to offer a sympathetic subversion of the concept.

And this is as important today as is was then, for haven't we been living under a similar illusion? That is, although we reject the image of the cold, distant analyst, there is a tendency to think one does that by adopting a more emotionally demonstrative relation with one's patients, perhaps by telling them more about how one feels oneself. This is the other side of the same coin. It rests on the assumption that if one is to reject the idea of the analyst as objective, one has no choice but to move over to a conception of the analyst as subjective (or intersubjective). Loewald's strategy is to help us grasp from the inside that we are not in fact prisoners of fixed concepts with absolutely determinate meanings. This does not mean that anything goes, but it does mean that we need to look at the various ways we live with a concept, rather than assume that a fixed meaning is forever imposed on us.

So rather than thinking that we are confronted with this exhaustive choice—*either* objective (dispassionate) *or* subjective (emotionally demonstrative)—we open up ways of thinking that allow us to open up new ways of living. We find that there are ways of being objective and dispassionate, yet emotionally engaged—emotionally engaged without thereby being demonstrative. We find ways to manifest our love precisely through a lack of emotional demonstration. It is this living possibility that opens up for us.

Is the psychoanalyst, then, essentially a lover? Freud said that psychoanalysis was a cure through love, but at least at the conscious level he was thinking of the use psychoanalysis makes of the patient's erotic transference.[9] But, then, what about the analyst? Is it only a question about whether the analyst also experiences erotic transferences toward her analysands? Or is it that the analyst sublimates her erotic energy in her analytic work? Perhaps she does some of the time, perhaps she does most of the time, perhaps she does all of the time, and though it is interesting to know, this kind of inquiry does not go very deep.

Rather than focusing on the feelings of the analyst, we should focus on her commitments. The commitments that interest us are the ones that constitute the psychoanalytic stance. To what extent are these commitments loving commitments? Here we are concerned not with the feeling of love but with its logic.[10]

---

9. Freud and Jung (1974, pp. 12–13).
10. I am particularly indebted to conversations with John Haugeland. Interested readers might wish to consult two of his essays (Haugeland 1998, 2000).

First, the analyst has an open-ended commitment to helping the analysand understand himself better, and to help him better understand the relationship they are in. Think of the parents with their child as they help draw her—through interpretations, questions, and attention—into the realm of meaning and self-understanding. Think also of adult lovers for whom the process of interpretation and reinterpretation—of coming to see things in a new light—is never at an end.

Second, the analyst is committed to facilitating the analysand's freedom. We may not know precisely what we mean by this—and it is also a hallmark of love that we are willing to live with a certain uncertainty about what we ultimately mean—but, in general, we are not interested in influencing our analysands to pursue any particular end, but in helping them to develop their own capacities for self-understanding, for understanding of others, and for thinking through what they want to do based on a better understanding of who they are and what they want.

Third, the analyst lives with a lively sense of death. That is, the analyst must live with a lively sense of what would bring this analysis to an end. Basically, there are two different types of endings: betrayal and termination. Let's start with betrayal. If we think of two lovers and ask ourselves what makes this relationship different from mere clinging, we begin to realize that there must be some events such that if they should occur, the love relationship will be at an end. The two people may stay together, they may even be bound by the superglue of emotional attachments, but whatever it is they may feel, they are no longer in love. A betrayed love is not describing one kind of love among others, it is describing a relationship that, in the dimension of love, has come undone.[11] Now part of a love relationship is a commitment to work to understand unfolding events in ways that preserve, even enhance, the love relationship. So part of being in love is manifest in the commitment to try to interpret an event as something other than a betrayal. Nevertheless, the love relationship is also committed to truthfulness, and there comes a point where one's ability honestly to understand an event in another light runs out.

This somewhat unfamiliar aspect of love plays a crucial role in psychoanalysis. It emerges in the form of an ever-present question: Is this analysis? No doubt some of the debates that have occurred within the profession have been petty squabbles, but they surround a constitutional question. Psychoanalysis is in part constituted by an ongoing debate on what psychoanalysis is. We may not know all the answers, but we constantly live with a sense of a boundary condition: *this* would betray the analysis. It is this commitment that keeps us focused on our task of promoting the analysand's freedom through the activity of interpretation and that keeps us from straying from that task by succumbing to some other emotional temptation. And here we see how love not only permits objectivity but also requires it.

---

11. To paraphrase Monty Python: a dead parrot isn't a way of being a parrot, it's a way of not being a parrot.

The other ending is termination, and the analyst should have it in sight (however inchoately) from the beginning. Think of parents who manifest their love for their child by facilitating the process by which the child grows up and becomes more independent. The love in parenting is manifest in the recognition from the beginning that parenting has its own termination phase. Other forms of love and intimacy may well grow into its place, but the parenting relation itself should be structured in such a way as to phase itself out. Should the parenting relation remain rigidly the same as the years pass, it ceases to be a manifestation of love and becomes another form of clinging. Similarly with psychoanalytic treatment. If psychoanalysis is aimed at promoting a person's freedom, part of the freedom is freedom from the need to keep coming to the analyst. It is a manifestation of love that the analyst, in her role as analyst, keeps an eye on that goal.

What does it mean to say that the analyst lives with a *lively* sense of death? Basically, it means that the analyst takes responsibility for maintaining the analysis as an analysis. In any love relationship there is at least an inchoate sense of death in it. Perhaps no one has explicitly thought about it, perhaps no one clearly knows, perhaps lovers are sure it could never happen to them, but for this to be love, rather than mere clinging, there has got to be at least an implicit and inchoate sense of what would be involved in its falling apart. But a psychoanalyst needs to take much greater responsibility for death. She has to keep present to her mind a vivid sense of what is involved in preserving and facilitating the analytic relationship. In part this is done by ever-renewed questioning of what would be involved in betraying it. She takes herself to be responsible for understanding what that betrayal would be, and for avoiding it. This is the way she maintains her commitment to being an analyst.[12]

She also takes responsibility for seeing the analysis through to its end. Some parents can naturally "let go" of their children when the time comes; for other parents, the idea of eventually letting go when the time comes was there from the beginning, structuring the way they acted as parents. In both cases we can imagine the parents having done well—in both cases we can imagine them loving and letting go. Yet in the latter case the parents took responsibility for letting go, and in this way the eventual letting go was always there as part of the relationship. In this sense, the end was always in sight. This is what I mean by a *lively* sense of death. Whatever you may think of this in terms of parenting, in analysis a lively sense of death is crucial. In terms of everything the analyst says or does in the analysis, it ought to be in the context of an ever-renewed questioning: How does *this* facilitate the analysis? Part of facilitating the analysis must be facilitating the analysis through to its end. Analysis is a relation-

---

12. This is analogous to Heidegger's distinction between being-toward-death (which is present in every love relationship) and authentic, resolute being-toward-death (in which a participant takes responsibility for his love).

ship with a termination, and it is only by keeping that in mind that the analyst can really answer the question of what does and does not facilitate the analysis.

Once we take these aspects of love seriously, we can see that the task of becoming a psychoanalyst is never at an end. For it is not simply that there is no end to the process of coming to understand another (and to understand oneself in the project of understanding another), of helping another come to understand himself, and of promoting another person's freedom. After all, in the name of freedom, analyses do come to an end, and we hope that analysands can then go off and lead better, freer lives. No, it is really the "till-death-do-us-part" condition that makes the project of becoming an analyst an infinite task. For we need constantly to keep alive a sense of what analysis is and what it isn't, and to take responsibility for that distinction in everything we do within our psychoanalytic work. This is a process that by its very nature cannot be a once-and-for-all achievement.

I said earlier that *psychoanalyst* should be understood as a subjective concept. We now have a much deeper sense of what that means. Becoming a psychoanalyst is a way of forming oneself as a subject, and the process of forming oneself as this kind of a subject, with those peculiar commitments of love, is never at an end. As a true psychoanalyst, one is always in the process of deepening oneself as a psychoanalyst. By now we are ready to understand the following claim without a tinge of paradox: the more subjective one becomes, the more objective one can be. For it is precisely as one deepens oneself as a psychoanalyst that one can ever better reach out to one's analysands in their objective particularity. That is, one can reach out to them as the subjects they are.

But to say that *psychoanalyst* should be understood as subjective does not mean that is how it *has* been understood. As it happens, the concept as it has been passed along through the generations has remained in an un–worked-out limbo of confusions and fantasies. There are fantasies of objectivity (that themselves could not possibly fit actual psychoanalytic activity) that are somehow mixed together with subjective commitments. The concept has not been worked through. We can see that even the term *psychoanalyst* can facilitate our own ambivalence. For what is it to be an *analyst* of the psyche? The English word "analysis" comes directly from the Greek *analusis*, which means to resolve or break something down into its constituent parts. In ancient Greece, the term was used in geometry to describe the process of starting with a complex geometrical figure and breaking it down step by step. The reverse process, synthesis, is the stepwise process of construction from simple elements that we are familiar with in Euclid's geometry. Also, Aristotle's logical works were called the *Analytics*, as they showed how arguments and proofs could be resolved into their constituent elements. By the nineteenth century, in which Freud wrote, the word had a significant use within chemistry to describe the process of resolving a chemical compound into its elements. One can see how these meanings of *analysis* could facilitate a misunderstanding of ourselves as objective analyzers of the psyche. Our interest in the analysand's psyche would be analogous to the chemist's interest in a chemical compound. In this way, we can disguise from ourselves the essential nature of our own engagement.

But there is another valence to analysis, and perhaps we can get to it if we push a bit at what we mean by "psyche." The translation of "psyche" into English is "soul." By and large, psychoanalysts begin to get uncomfortable when someone tells them they are analysts of the soul,[13] perhaps because we think that the word *soul* has ineluctable religious connotations. But, then, why do we need to think that? And do we really know what we are thinking when we think that? We need to overcome this split and acknowledge that insofar as we are committed to understanding the psyche, we are committed to understanding the soul, for (whatever it may be precisely) a soul is just what a psyche is. Admittedly, it becomes more difficult to apply a chemical analogy to our relation to another person's soul. And now, it seems, *analysis* can take on a more subjective meaning. The reason we insist on being psycho*analysts* is not to hide behind a white lab coat in our dealings with others, but rather to remind ourselves that our commitment is to promoting psychological freedom. We avoid suggesting this or that outcome to our analysands, avoid moralizing, avoid telling them that they really will be happy if only they achieve this particular social goal. In that sense, we are not in the business of psyche-synthesis. At best,

---

13. See, for example, Bruno Bettelheim (1983).

we try to facilitate a process in which the analysands can engage in psyche-synthesis for themselves. We help others come to better understand themselves, but how they go on with that better understanding is up to them.

Here is Loewald's diagnosis of the origins of our confusion:

> Involved in the insistence that the analytic activity is a strictly scientific one (not merely using scientific knowledge and methods) is the notion of the dignity of science. Scientific man is considered by Freud as the most advanced form of human development. The scientific stage of development of man's conception of the universe has its counterpart in the individual's state of maturity, according to *Totem and Taboo*. Scientific self-understanding to which the patient is helped, is in and by itself therapeutic, following this view, since it implies the movement towards a stage of human evolution not previously reached. The patient is led towards the maturity of scientific man who understands himself and external reality not in animistic or religious terms but in terms of objective science. There is little doubt that what we call the scientific exploration of the universe, including the self, may lead to greater mastery over it (within certain limits of which we are becoming painfully aware). The activity of mastering it, however, is not itself a scientific activity. If scientific objectivity is assumed to be the most mature stage of man's understanding of the universe, indicating the highest degree of the individual's state of maturity, we may have a vested inter-

est in viewing psychoanalytic therapy as a purely scientific activity and its effects as due to such scientific objectivity. Beyond the issue of a vested interest, I believe it to be necessary and timely to question the assumption, handed to us from the nineteenth century, that the scientific approach to the world and the self represents a higher and more mature evolutionary stage of man than the religious way of life. But I cannot pursue this question here.[14]

This passage is so wise, and its wisdom so moving, that we can easily overlook the argumentative strategy. This was an astonishing paragraph to write in a professional journal aimed mainly at medical doctors emerging from the 1950s. But if it continues to pack a punch, that is because it brings us back to our own commitments. In effect, Loewald offers us an interpretation in which we are invited to see, embarrassingly enough, the phenomenon of transference at work in the formation of our own identities as analysts. The fact that we have a vested interest in viewing psychoanalysis as a purely scientific activity means, in effect, that we have a temptation to view ourselves as engaged in scientific activity—even though we have only the most rudimentary sense of what that might be. We have fallen in love with a self-image instead of coming to understand ourselves as falling under a concept.

---

14. Loewald (1960), op. cit., p. 228.

It's not going to be of help simply to say that we
don't think of ourselves as scientists anymore. If we don't
know what is involved in being a scientist, then we have
no idea what was involved in giving it up. If there was
confusion in our previous self-understanding, we are
likely to preserve some confusion if we simply reject it.
When we are analyzing individuals we know that an
analysand cannot simply reject his past. Such a purported
rejection will only lead to an unconscious repetition.
Rather, the analysand needs to work through his past if
he is to move on in new and fresh ways. Something similar is true in our life with concepts.

One needs to hold onto the original aspiration and
see what its deeper meanings could be. We claim to be
psychoanalysts, and that claim immediately entangles us
in a set of commitments, the full meanings of which are
as yet beyond our grasp. Even at the conceptual level,
there is a significant unconscious dimension involved in
being a psychoanalyst. We try to make our commitments
clear to ourselves by conceiving of ourselves as scientists.
But then Loewald (and others) help us to recognize a
significant defensive dimension in our identification.
What next?

One route is to hold onto the thought of science
and ask what it could possibly mean. Let us suppose a
scientist to be someone who pursues inquiry into an area
by means that are appropriate for yielding knowledge
about that subject matter. We have already seen that *scientist* is a subjective concept: a scientist is someone who
shapes herself as a subject by the ever-renewed commit-

ment to inquiring into a certain realm in appropriate ways. The true scientist, then, will not just be inquiring into a certain realm, she will also be inquiring into the best ways of inquiring into that realm. This is a never-ending commitment. Indeed, I constitute myself as a scientist to some extent by keeping myself open to changing how I investigate a given realm, in light of better understandings of what it would be to yield knowledge in that realm. It is essential to being a scientist that I ever be engaged with the question of how to live as a scientist. What counts as scientific is the activity of a scientist who behaves appropriately as such.

But now we can see that the claim that the psychoanalyst is a scientist is in one sense true and in another sense is a confusion. In the confused version, we take the idea of science as absolutely fixed, even if we don't have a clear idea of what that allegedly fixed idea is. For example, we take the image of the physicist of the nineteenth century and try to transfer the dignity of his rigor over to psychoanalysis. Since we don't have a clear idea of what his activity consisted of, we are likely to remain ignorant of all the difficulties that would be involved if we were genuinely to try to adapt the methods of that realm of inquiry to an inquiry into the human psyche. What does the inquiry into the atomic structure of helium have to do with an inquiry into the human attempt to make meaning? It is a sign that we were motivated to live in confusion that we tended to avoid such questions.

It is not going to help simply to get hip with science. That is, if we now start talking about indeterminacy or relativity, aren't we still doing essentially the same thing—latching onto an idealized image of a science we don't really understand? And yet it also seems misguided to flip to the other side and say that this conception of psychoanalysis as a science is false. That would suggest that there is a determinate idea here, which turns out not to be true, and, having discovered that, we could go on and declare that psychoanalysis is *not* a science, assuming all along (on both sides of the affirmation and denial) that we knew what we were talking about. This is one way in which thinking gets emptied of thought. Much better to recognize that we live amidst confused and idealized images. That then frees us up to investigate how psychoanalysis might actually be a science after all.

The movement of thought Loewald's writing inspires is a kind of conceptual therapy, and its name is irony. I am reluctant to invoke the i-word because it is so often misunderstood. Indeed, the irony about irony is that it is almost impossible to find out what it means. At least, it is almost impossible using standard resources—a dictionary, encyclopedia, or introductory article—to come to understand the deeper and most significant meaning of the concept. For example, the dictionary gives us an account of prevalent uses of the term. But if the prevalent uses are themselves confused, there is every reason to suspect that the confusions will be preserved in the dictionary entries. The philosopher Ludwig Wittgenstein talked of the folly of buying a second copy of the newspaper to check on the accuracy of what the first copy says. We don't realize it, but that is often what we are doing when we see the word *irony* mentioned in a book, and get up and go to the dictionary. For the lexicographer is only trying to work out meaning from standard usages, perhaps from the very passage you are reading, and if the author is himself confused, how is the lexicographer to know?

Even worse, you may be reading a deep passage about irony—say, from Plato or Kierkegaard—but when you go to the dictionary you find an entry based on much shallower, even confused, uses. In this way, going to the dictionary can make things worse, for now you think you understand the term and you go back and misread the passage.

This problem tends to get compounded with the introductory essay, because the essay typically begins with dictionary definitions. Thus the confusion in the dictionary gets taken up in the introductory exposition. To extend Wittgenstein's analogy, this is like buying a third copy of the newspaper to get clear on what was in the second.

It feels like *no exit!* And what's especially confusing about all this is, as it were, that a million people can't be wrong. That is, if the word *irony* comes to take on a confused and superficial set of meanings, then, eventually, this is what the word comes to mean. In this sense, the dictionary cannot be completely wrong. Yet, precisely because it must be right about this confused and superficial use, we hide from ourselves the deeper meaning of what irony is really all about. We hide from ourselves why irony matters.

So, for example, the *Shorter Oxford English Dictionary* defines irony as "a figure of speech in which the intended meaning is the opposite as that expressed by the words used; usually taking the form of sarcasm or ridicule in which laudatory expressions are used to express condemnation or contempt."[15] There are two important problems with this definition. First, irony is importantly different from sarcasm, which you would never know by reading the definition. In his pioneering article, "Irony in Psychoanalysis," Martin Stein gives this as an example of irony[16]:

Analyst: I have your bill ready.
Patient: Fantastic.

This, I want to argue, is not irony, though it is sarcasm. Stein himself describes the situation this way: "My remark, 'I have your bill ready,' was literal and straightforward, allowing of no other meaning. My patient's reply, 'Fantastic!' was clearly ironic, and would be so understood by any person familiar with analysis. The speaker did not imply that he was thrilled at being presented with a bill— quite the contrary; he intended that I should understand him in a sense opposite to the literal expression."[17]

---

15. *The Shorter Oxford English Dictionary on Historical Principles*, third edition. W. Little, H. W. Fowler, J. Coulson, C. T. Onions, eds. Oxford: 1972, vol. 1, p. 1045.
16. Stein (1985). See also the very insightful article by Roy Schafer (1970).
17. Stein, op. cit., p. 37.

Of course, given the dictionary definition, this is a perfect example of irony. But, perhaps ironically, the dictionary definition has itself been duped. One way to become healthily uncomfortable with the definition is to ask oneself this question: How could some of the greatest minds of all time—Socrates, Plato, Kierkegaard, for example—be so interested in irony if this is all it meant? A clever and sadistic professor might say, "Fine exam, Mr. Jones" as he hands back a flunking grade, but is Socratic irony really so flat-footed as that? Note, too, that if this is what irony amounts to within an analytic situation, then there is little more to do with it than analyze it as a specific defensive form of humor. Interesting in its own terms, but not particularly deep.

This leads to the second problem with this dictionary entry: in a proper use of irony there is no reason to think "the intended meaning is the opposite expressed by the words used." In the above example, "Fantastic" is used sarcastically to mean *not* fantastic. But, as we shall see, what is so special about irony is that the words are used to mean exactly what they do mean. Indeed, the irony becomes possible precisely because the speaker insists on holding onto what the words really do mean. How is this possible?

To see how, we need to go to one of the great thinkers on irony and refrain from imposing a dictionary definition on him. Instead of assuming that we already know what irony is, and then reading him through that lens, let's let him speak to us more directly. In this way we shall come to see what a crucial role irony plays in the therapeutic process.

Consider this entry from Kierkegaard's *Diary*:

> Basically my whole existence is the deepest irony.
>
> Going to South America, descending into subterranean caverns to dig up remains of vanished animal forms and antediluvian fossils: there is nothing ironical about that, for animals one comes across today living in such places do not, after all, pretend to be the same as the ancient ones.
>
> But plumb the middle of "Christendom" to want to excavate the foundation of what it means to be a Christian, which bears almost the same relation to our contemporary Christians as the bones of the ancient animals to those now living: that is the most intense irony. The irony is that while Christianity is supposed to exist there are at the same time thousands of prelates in velvet, silks and broadcloth, millions of Christians begetting Christians, etc.
>
> What did Socrates' irony actually consist of? Could it be certain terms and turns of speech or such? No, these are mere trifles; maybe virtuosity in speaking ironically? Such things do not constitute a Socrates. No, his entire life was irony and consisted of this: while the whole contemporary population of farm-stewards, trades people etc., in brief, these thousands, while all of them were absolutely sure that they were human beings and knew what it meant to be a human being, Socrates

probed in depth (ironically) and busied himself with
the problem: *what does it mean to be a human being?* By
doing so he really expressed that all the bustle [*trieben*]
of these thousands was an illusion, a phantasmagoria, a
tumult, a noise a bustle. . . . Socrates doubted that a
person was a human being at birth; it doesn't come so
easy, and neither does the knowledge of what it means
to be a human being."[18]

Irony is made possible by a peculiar entanglement of life,
pretense, and language. Kierkegaard, a religious figure,
is living with the question, What is it to be a Christian?
This is not our question now. But we can see ourselves
living with an analogous question, What is it to be a
psychoanalyst? Or: What is therapeutic action? For
Kierkegaard, it is a confusion to think that one can become a Christian by falling in with currently accepted
practices. One is baptized a Christian in the local church,
goes to church on Sundays, marries another such person in the church, brings one's children to be baptized
in the same church, and so on. To think that one can
look to these facts about oneself in order to be able to
say, "Yes, I am a Christian," is, for Kierkegaard, an illusion. For it is precisely this kind of reassurance that keeps
one, unbeknownst to oneself, at a distance from Christianity. It is as though the term *Christian* serves as a defense, keeping one unaware that there is any further issue
involved in being a Christian. And yet, though the word

---

18. Kierkegaard (1960, § 163, pp. 128–129).

Christian has become entangled in elaborate contemporary rituals, it still seems to hang onto some underlying aspiration. Thus it is possible for Kierkegaard to ask, "Is there a single Christian in all of Christendom?" And it is possible for us to recognize that there is a real question here, even if we don't fully know what the question means. *Christian*: we recognize a tension within the word itself, a tension between its pretenses and its aspirations, such that if we were to grasp both sides of that tension, we would undergo a transformation of the psyche.

Human being: On the one hand there is an easy answer to the question, "Am I a human being?" There are certain objective facts about me that guarantee that the answer is yes: my parents were of the biological species *homo sapiens*; I was born into that species; ergo, I'm human. But for Socrates, *human being* is a subjective category: I should ever be in the process of becoming human by shaping myself into a person who lives a distinctively human life. There is no fixed answer as to what this means. And while alive, there is no end to the task. There are intimations of this subjective sense in ordinary language. For example, at universities we have humanities divisions, and these divisions typically leave out the ordinary empirical studies of human beings, like sociology, anthropology, and psychology. Rather, they try to present to us the finest works of literature, philosophy, and art, that is, what the culture regards as the greatest attempts to express what it is to be human. This has got to be human in the subjective sense. To take another example, Americans of European descent, particularly Jews, will

on occasion say of someone that he or she is a real *Mensch*.
The meaning is that they are real human beings in the
subjective sense: they incorporate their sense of human-
ity into their daily lives. And, of course, the marvelous
Judge Schreber, who in his psychotic wisdom, gave psychoanalysis so much to think about, had the category of
the "fleetingly improvised person": as though most
people around him were in fact hastily constructed shells
to give the appearance of human life. There is, as we all
know, much truth in Herr Schreber's madness.[19]

Note in both these examples the utter lack of sarcasm. When Kierkegaard asks, "Is there a Christian in all
of Christendom?" it's a real question. He doesn't mean
the opposite, i.e., *non*-Christian, by his use of "Christian."
(By contrast, the patient really does mean *not* fantastic
by his use of "fantastic.") Rather, Kierkegaard fastens onto
a deep meaning, a true meaning of Christian, which
members of Christendom can themselves recognize as a
true meaning, even if they only inchoately understand
it. Although the members of Christendom, for the most
part, may take their Christianity for granted, and although they may for the most part assume it is expressed
in various outward rituals, like baptism and going to
church, they can also hear the call of Kierkegaard's question, because, however inchoately, they recognize that it

---

19. See Daniel Paul Schreber (1903). Freud gives Schreber credit
for inventing, in his own psychotic fantasies, a theory of his relations with God that bears an uncanny relation to Freud's own li-
bido theory. See Freud (1911).

is part of the very meaning of *Christian*, that it expresses an aspiration that transcends the many outward, objective practices. These are, quite literally, *pretenses* to Christianity, but even in the midst of them, one can still hear the call of the aspiration.

Furthermore, even though Kierkegaard may be confident that the various outward trappings of Christianity do not themselves answer his question, that is, he knows that one can't answer his question in the affirmative simply because he sees someone going to church, nevertheless, for him it remains a genuine question. It is not as though he is asking a question to which he himself already knows the answer, but is going to make you guess. Rather, he sees that actively living with the question of what it is to be a Christian is part of his own process of becoming/being a Christian. The question is an intensely real one for him.

H. W. Fowler, in his magnificent *A Dictionary of Modern English Usage*, gives an esoteric account of irony: "The word *irony* which in its more general sense may be defined as the use of words intended to convey one meaning to the uninitiated part of the audience and another to the initiated, the delight of it lying in the secret intimacy set up between the latter and the speaker."[20] On this account, Kierkegaard would already have some esoteric understanding of being a Christian that he was nodding and winking to the cognoscenti, just as he continued to bewilder and confuse the vulgar and uninitiated. Ob-

---

20. Fowler (1926, p. 296).

viously, there are certain remarks that can fit this scheme, but it is a gross mischaracterization of Kierkegaard's irony. First, it is essential to Kierkegaard that he himself is living with the question. For him, to suppose oneself to possess the esoteric answer is to subvert the ever-renewing process of living with the question. Second, it would be anathema to Kierkegaard's own understanding of Christianity to turn his back on anyone, however simple, who he might otherwise help in their process of becoming a Christian. And the idea of taking delight in their ignorance, or parading their ignorance before the cognoscenti for their delight, well, for him, that would be the sin of pride.

Indeed, Kierkegaard's use of irony here is meant to be therapeutic. In asking whether there is a Christian in all of Christendom, he is asking people to recognize their own unease. At some level, however inchoately, the members of Christendom themselves understand that their Christianity is not settled simply by the outward gesture of going to church. This is somehow already part of their own understanding of Christianity. In that sense, the irony is not meant for the esoteric to delight in, it is meant to help "the vulgar" come to realize they already have a question, when before they thought they had the answers.

Similarly with the Socratic question, "Among the citizens of Athens, is there a human being?" The second entry for irony in the *Oxford English Dictionary* is *feigned ignorance*, which the dictionary attributes to Socrates. To be fair, the dictionary definition does not come from nowhere. Socrates nowhere says that he himself is ironic—being ironic is a charge his interlocutors level against him.[21] They accuse him of it when they get angry and frustrated in the debate, and they are accusing him of feigned ignorance. But why think that Socrates' debating partners have gotten it right? Not only have they misunderstood Socrates, they have misunderstood what irony is. The irony is that Socrates *is* ironic, but not at all in the way his interlocutors think.

When he asks, "What is involved in becoming truly human?" he is asking what would be the highest development of ourselves, what is the most noble and fine in becoming a human being, and how can we in the deepest sense become ourselves? Socrates recognizes that living with these questions—genuinely living with these questions as continually renewed questions—is a lifetime task. It is of the essence of Socratic irony that the question is a genuine question, which Socrates himself shares. From Socrates' point of view, if he thought he had the answer and only feigned ignorance, he would in fact have already given up on the project of becoming human. For living with the question is of the essence of becoming (being) human.

Note that we hear the call of Socrates' question precisely because we resonate to a deep meaning of *human being*, which, however inchoately, we already recognize.

---

21. For a discussion of this, see Gregory Vlastos (1991). I am afraid that Vlastos's own analysis is compromised by an overreliance on dictionary definitions of what irony is, but it does lay out the textual evidence clearly.

Socrates isn't using *human being* to mean the opposite—as the sarcastic analysand uses "fantastic" to mean *not* fantastic. He is, as it were, drawing our attention to a deep meaning of *human being,* which is already our meaning. Though we may usually take the category of human being for granted, the irony helps us recognize that we are already attuned to an aspiration, even if no one can fully say what the aspiration is.

Freud used the category of the human as an unsorted-out amalgam of objective and subjective uses, and thus he has been open for a wide range of interpretations. Those who wish to stress the essentially subjective nature of psychoanalysis—that it is essentially concerned with the development of the subject—will focus on Freud's dawning realization that the psyche is itself a psychological achievement. "A unity comparable to the ego (or the I) cannot exist in the individual from the start," says Freud in "On Narcissism." And he sees that "a new psychical action is required" for an I to come into existence.[22] This would seem to leave open the possibility that the I is ever in the process of development. Indeed, Freud suggests this when he lays down his memorable phrase for the task of psychoanalysis: "Where id was, there ego shall be."[23] Or, more accurately and more hauntingly: "Where it was there I shall become." This would seem to suggest that the project

22. Freud (1914, p. 77). See also Freud (1929, chapter 1).
23. Freud (1932, p. 80).

of becoming an I is the essential human task, and that psychoanalysis is an integral part of that project.

Yet in those very same pages, the I will be treated as though it were a quasi-biological entity.[24] There are times when he suggests that he resorts to psychology simply because the state of biology is not sufficiently advanced, as though one day there will be a purely biological account of the development of the I. This is the kind of confusion that promotes more confusion. Consider a contemporary example: the interest among psychoanalysts in the current state of brain research.

Let me say loud and clear: I am all in favor of neuroscientific research. And I am strongly in favor of figuring out what insights neuroscience might lend to psychoanalysis.[25] If we look back to Freud's early work on aphasia, we can see that his efforts to chart brain function and dysfunction did have significant influence on his subsequent formulation of psychoanalysis.[26] If we try to look forward, we should accept that we simply cannot say ahead of time what creative insights neuroscience and psychoanalysis might jointly yield.

But one also needs to recognize that however legitimate the interest in neuroscience, there is also a defen-

---

24. See in particular Freud (1914), op. cit., and Freud (1920). See also Frank J. Sulloway (1979).
25. See Mark Solms and Oliver Turnbull (2002); Regina Pally (2000); Mark Solms (1997).
26. See Freud (1953); Ana-Maria Rizzuto (1993); Mark Solms and Michael Saling (1986).

sive use to which that interest can be put. The defense is to use neuroscience as yet another idealized image of a science that psychoanalysis can latch onto in order to claim legitimacy for itself. The reasoning goes something like this: Psychoanalysis has to take neurological research seriously if it is going to be true to itself as an objective science. But if psychoanalysis is an objective science, it must be continuous with its fellow objective science, neuroscience. In that case, it is at least conceivable, as Freud himself seems to have believed, that neuroscience may one day replace psychoanalysis. Or, perhaps, that psychoanalysis may one day develop into its own branch of neuroscience. That seems to be the cost of accepting that psychoanalysis is a science. If it is not a science, then, the thought goes, it is merely subjective, and thus anything goes. As though I can give my interpretation, you can give yours, for, after all, the art of interpretation is merely subjective, meaning is indeterminate, and so on.

What a mess! But the mess isn't revealed in any one particular belief; it is revealed in a mistaken view of the universe of possibilities. For the underlying assumption seems to be, "Either objective (in which case continuous with and replaceable by neuroscience) or merely subjective," as though there are no other possibilities than these.

By now it should be clear that the right response is not to choose one side or the other but to dissolve this dilemma. To say that psychoanalysis is essentially a subjective endeavor is not to say that it has no interest in objectivity; we have already seen the sense in which it is important to strive toward objectivity in our dealings with our patients. It may also take up the latest results in neuroscience in all sorts of unforeseen ways. But insofar as it does so, it should always be under the overarching question, How does this help us in the overall project of facilitating the development of the subject?

Consider, by way of example, a familiar situation in contemporary psychopharmacology: the prescription of an antidepressant. It may be of inestimable help to know the neurochemistry of the brain–drug interactions. If we know on the neurobiological level what lifting a depression looks like, we may, for instance, be able to see what other areas of brain activity are also affected. We may be able to choose among drugs for differences that are detectable only at the micro, not at the macro, level. We cannot tell ahead of time what the discoveries will be and what they will mean.

Nevertheless, from a psychoanalytic perspective, the point of the antidepressant is not simply to relieve the pain and lift the depression; it is to help to put the patient back into a position where she can again take up the task of developing herself as a subject. But there is no drug, now or ever, that can perform that task.

It is the idea that antidepressants can replace psychoanalysis that is a confusion. For it is to treat a person as though she were only a biological organism—a collation of nerves and tissues—as though there were no issue of what it is for her to develop as a person. Of course, the profession of psychoanalysis itself facilitated this confusion via its own scientistic self-misunderstanding. It advertised itself as offering a cure for depression. Thus when a better psychopharmacological type of cure comes along, there is every reason to ask, Why do we need to hold onto that old-fashioned medicine? The confusion is compounded by the fact that for certain patients and certain forms of depression, psychoanalysis *does* help lift the depression. The thought is inevitable: Why not just treat everyone with the cheaper, more universally effective drug?

Lifting a depression can make a huge difference in how a person is able to live her life. The problem only arises if one assumes that, having lifted the depression, there is no further question about how to live. It is as though *human being* is a fixed objective category: Before, this human was in a depression. Now the depression is lifted. End of story. That is how one forgets to be a human being.

Here is a healthier psychoanalytic attitude toward depression: certain depressions are themselves the outcome of fundamental neurotic conflicts occurring deep within a person's psyche. As a person comes to a deeper understanding of who she is, and, in particular, as she comes to resolve that conflict, one should expect the depression to lift. Other depressions are not like this, and we may not know much about them other than that they are caused by chemical imbalances and can be shifted by correcting those imbalances. It would be inappropriate to try to cure these depressions simply by talking. Nevertheless, these depressions are not only the effects of certain causes but also the causes of other effects—and some of them occur deep within the psyche.

That is, even if a chemical imbalance causes one's depression, one will tend to make meanings around this depression. There will be fantasies about what these feelings mean *for me*. One might say that, whether we like it or not, we are always in the business of becoming human. We are making meanings about who we are, what things mean for us, which in fact shapes who we are. Much of this occurs unconsciously, beyond the range of our awareness or immediate control. Even if meanings did not fundamentally cause the depression, the depression will be causing meanings, and one needs to grasp these meanings if one wants to grasp the life one is living.

How do we fail to notice this? How could the existence of an antidepressant make psychoanalysis seem obsolete? In part, as we have seen, psychoanalysis forgot that it was a science of the subject, and advertised itself as a medical cure for a specific disease. But our culture is fascinated with scientific research because it taps our futuristic fantasies. After all, if a drug can lift a depression today, who knows what's just around the corner! No doubt marvelous treatments await us, and some of them will impact psychoanalytic treatment in unpredictable ways. Still, the idea that drugs might—if not now, soon!— take the place of psychoanalysis is comparable to thinking that drugs may one day replace the task each of us faces of becoming the kind of person we should each like to be.

When it comes to technology, the "if not now, soon" fantasy is so pervasive in contemporary American culture that a healthy antidote, at least for a moment, is to step outside the culture and outside the times. Johannes Climacus reminds us of a time in midnineteenth century Europe when serious scholars were trying to prove by objective means that Jesus was indeed the son of God.[27] Climacus shows us that no matter how many facts we pile up about the historical Jesus—what the witnesses said, the miracles reported—about the composition of the Bible, and so on, they could not possibly settle the question of faith. For the kinds of facts that an historian can genuinely compile, the kinds of evidence he can amass, the kind of knowing that objective historical knowledge consists in—well, it is simply not the sort stuff that could ever settle the question of whether Jesus is the son of God. We know right now that no matter what an archaeological dig turns up in Bethlehem, it is not going to settle that issue; nor will it help to move the dig to Jerusalem. The truth of Jesus is not an objective issue in this sense.

The researchers keep themselves from seeing this by imagining that the real discovery is around the corner, if only they keep up the research. And herein lies the possibility of irony. The researchers take themselves to be engaged in a spectacular research project, as though they have an idea in their heads of what it would take to complete it. Climacus compares this research project to a great engineering project of his day: building a tunnel under the Thames River in London.[28] That project,

---

27. Kierkegaard (1846), op. cit., book one.
28. Ibid., p. 26.

begun in 1825, encountered disasters and setbacks along the way, but was finally completed in 1845. The historical researchers take themselves to be involved in a project like that—long and arduous, having many setbacks, but one that will eventually reach its goal. But, then, what is it about the tunnelers that makes it true to say that they are digging a tunnel rather than, say, just playing around in the mud? They can truly be said to be digging a tunnel because they have a fixed goal in mind—a point on the other side of the Thames where they mean to emerge—and a set of practical skills that makes it reasonable for them to suppose that, with effort and some cooperation from nature, they can make it.

There are two different ways this analogy can break down. The first is if the means to achieving the goal are wildly inadequate to the task. Put a three-year-old with a plastic cup on the bank of the Thames, and no matter what he says he is doing, he is not digging a tunnel to the other side. Similarly, no jump I take, no matter how earnest, could possibly be an attempt to jump to the moon. But even so, the three-year-old and I might both have some vague idea of what it would be to succeed. The second is if there is no conceivable idea of what could count as succeeding. If there were no point on the other side of the river, if there was nothing in virtue of which one could be said to be digging in the right direction rather than the wrong direction, then the idea that one was digging a tunnel would be sheer pretence. This is the situation the historians are in when they take themselves to be burrowing toward God.

In a similar vein, we may learn much about the brain that is of value in alleviating human suffering, in figuring out how to alter unwanted moods, and in finding out how emotions are correlated to certain brain states, but none of this can answer the subjective question: What is it *for me* to become a person? This is a question that cannot be answered by looking at my brain states—even looking next year, when we will know so much more about the brain than we do today. Rather, we should need to know more about what I love, more about what I could come to love, more about what I hate and could come to hate. Correlatively, we should need to know what it would be for me to betray that love—or to have that love betrayed. Psychoanalysis is alive because there is no straightforward or direct ways to answer these questions. In the proper sense of the term, they are essentially subjective questions. That is, I form myself as a subject by my living engagement with them. Neuroscience cannot answer those questions for me (not now or ever); psychoanalysis is (and will remain) essential. For there are inevitably aspects of my commitments that escape my conscious awareness, escape the immediate control of my conscious will. Psychoanalysis is a process by which I come to take responsibility for hitherto unconscious aspects of myself. I thereby deepen myself as a subject. My wishes and fantasies are taken into the orbit of my ongoing quest to become/be a person.

In the preface to his collected essays, Hans Loewald wrote: "Philosophy has been my first love. I gladly affirm its influence on my way of thinking while being wary of the peculiar excesses a philosophical bent tends to entail. My teacher in this field was Martin Heidegger, and I am deeply grateful for what I learned from him, despite his most hurtful betrayal in the Nazi era, which alienated me from him permanently."[29] Note the irony: on the one hand, Heidegger is the greatest philosopher of his time—the pretense to philosophy is there—and, on the other hand, what he is doing is so unwise. The philosopher—literally the one who loves wisdom—is living a life that attacks wisdom. The word *philosophy* is a manifestation of the illness and a pointer toward the cure. Heidegger is *the* philosopher, and his work at its best is of an astonishing depth. Yet, Heidegger's becoming a Nazi is not some quirky, split-off part of the self. Even if it is difficult to say how the thought and life interact, the philosophy and the man emerge as of a piece. Loewald's point is that there must be something wrong with this way of doing philosophy—whatever it is—if the thinking can also permit or facilitate becoming a Nazi.

Heidegger's most important work, *Being and Time*, concerns itself with the phenomenon of care. But how could this great work on the nature of care be written by someone who had become so careless? Isn't this Heidegger's own practical contradiction? The answer can't be to find out some more facts about care or even to study philosophically the overall structure of care. Rather, one has to learn to live more carefully. Might this have had

---

29. Loewald (2000), op. cit., pp. xlii–xliii.

something to do with Loewald's becoming a doctor: that
one thereby has the opportunity to shape oneself into a
person who cares in special kinds of ways? In this sense,
doctor is subjective category. To be a doctor, in the deepest
sense, one must ever commit oneself to becoming the sort
of person who can care for others in the right sorts of
ways. Properly understood, this is a never-ending task. It is
a process that shapes one's own psyche. As a doctor acquires and maintains her skills, she also looks out on the
world in a distinctive way. Part of becoming a doctor is
forming the right sense of medical objectivity. In making
a good diagnosis, one sees the world aright.

This would suggest that the search for wisdom is a
risky business. For if we generalize from the model of
becoming a doctor, it would seem that if we are search-
ing for wisdom, we find it not by finding the right object,
but by becoming the right kind of subject. Only when
one becomes the right kind of subject will one see the
world with the appropriate objectivity. (Only when we
become a doctor can we *see* the illness in the patient.)
But what if one throws oneself into the wrong sort of
activity? By the time one can judge it, one's perspective
is also skewed.[30] Consider, for example, the selfish person who looks out on the world and sees that *everyone else*
is selfish: they are all grabbing too much for themselves,
so she feels the need to grab her "fair share."

---

30. This problem flows directly from Plato's and Aristotle's theories of character development. See Plato *Republic* II–III; Aristotle,
Nicomachean Ethics, I–IV.

Or, closer to home, consider the person who is sure that talking cures are obsolete, and that some day psychopharmacology will be the only kind of treatment there is. Ironically he may be right; precisely because so many people believe this, as a *social fact* it may come true. But this does not mean that the problem of becoming a human being has been solved; it is rather that one more way of evading it has been invented. Of course, that is not how it will look to him.

In this section we have been concerned with the skewed perspectives that can arise within one's own attempt to become a psychoanalyst. And in this case at least, the form of therapy has been irony. In our own attempts to become analysts, we find ourselves perched between pretense and aspiration. On the one hand, there are the training programs at our institutes, our daily lives with patients, and so on; on the other hand, there seems to be something left open in the aspiration to be an analyst of the psyche. We recognize that however thorough our training, however careful our efforts, there is always room for the question, "Am I really being a psychoanalyst?" And we recognize that the answer to *that* question can never be, "Yes, because I graduated from the institute." And that's not because the right answer is, "Yes, because I am certified by the American Psychoanalytic Association." We recognize that the word itself—*psychoanalyst*—pulls us out of whatever contemporary embedding it has. It gives us at least the glimpse of a question of whether its contemporary realization is adequate to its aspiration.

We can't clearly recognize what this aspiration is. To do that would require that we had already changed ourselves as subjects—already undergone the shifts that would entail a shift of perspective. But we can feel the pull, and this is the tug of irony.

Similarly with the question, "Is this a therapeutic action?" In the first instance we may feel we can answer the question in the affirmative if our proposed intervention fits with the theory of, say, Hans Loewald—or Paul Gray, or Melanie Klein, or Jacques Lacan, or Anna Freud, or Sigmund Freud. We may think the answer is yes if it fits with current fashion, with what we have picked up from our training, conversations with colleagues, and so on. Yet there is something about that question that pulls us out of every context. It confronts us straight out with the question, Is *this* action genuinely therapeutic? A lifetime can be shaped around trying to answer such a question.

3

Internalization

Psychoanalyst is a subjective category: the process of shaping oneself into a psychoanalyst is one that never comes to an end. One is constantly learning from one's analysands, from other analysts, and from the interpretation and reinterpretation of what is going on with oneself and with others. This is not simply the exercise of the capacity (or set of capacities) to be a psychoanalyst—in the sense that once that capacity is established, all one need do is exercise it. Rather, the capacity itself is always being shaped, deepened, and extended. One might say that the processes of internalization by which one acquires the capacity to be a psychoanalyst never come to an end. Paradoxically, part of the internalization of the capacity to be a psychoanalyst is the recognition that this process of internalization must always be incomplete.

By contrast, consider learning to tie one's shoes. Before one has acquired the capacity, it seems like the most marvelous, yet almost unapproachable, task. But once one acquires the capacity, the magic soon fades, and the activity becomes automatic. Clearly, the repeated tying of one's shoes reinforces the capacity and keeps it alive. But there is no question of deepening or expanding the capacity. One has internalized the capacity—that's done—and now one can tie one's shoes.

The capacity to be a psychoanalyst is essentially not like that. It is a mistake to think of it as just a more complicated version of the same kind of capacity-acquisition: we go through a complicated training process, which includes our own analysis, course work, and the supervised analyses of others, and in that training process we acquire a settled capacity to analyze others as well as ourselves. For to be a psychoanalyst is ever to be in the process of becoming a psychoanalyst, and should we ever think that process is completed, either we are mistaken about ourselves or we have become psychoanalytic zombies—going through the motions of psychoanalysis and making appropriate noises, but dead at the center.

Consider, by way of analogy, the category of *doctor*. Clearly, there are subjective and objective uses of the concept *doctor*. Subjectively speaking, a doctor is a person who through medical knowledge brings health to others. One can ever be in the process of shaping oneself as a subject by a lifetime pursuit of the question of what constitutes health for humans, what is it to bring health to humans, how to dedicate oneself to others in health-giving ways. Objectively, a doctor is someone who has graduated successfully from a medical school, has a diploma hanging on his wall, and has been certified by the appropriate professional board and licensed in her state. Now when we go looking for a doctor, we hope we will find someone who fits both the subjective and the objective criteria for being a doctor. We recognize that if all we find is someone who has the objective trappings, we are probably not going to be well taken care of. But precisely because there is a gap between subjective and objective uses, there is room for a question, ironic as it is earnest, Is there a doctor in the American Medical Association? I am sure that the answer is yes, but precisely because there is a subjective use, we can see that the answer is not a truism. It is not true by definition that the American Medical Association is full of doctors (subjectively speaking).

Or consider the category of surgeon. For a significant period in European medical history, the answer to the question, Is a surgeon a doctor? was a resounding no! Going to the surgeon was like going to the barber—indeed, it regularly *was* going to the barber, though the procedure was usually more painful and less successful than getting one's hair cut. Still, the social implication was that surgery was mere technique. Perhaps the skills might change, and one may want to keep up with new techniques, but there was no particular implication that by learning those techniques one would be developing oneself as a subject. But once the category of surgeon is absorbed into the category of doctor, there arise two ways to understand the claim that surgeons are doctors. Objectively, the question is settled because surgery is a branch of official medicine, taught at medical schools, and accredited by professional associations. Subjectively, the question is whether a surgeon has allowed his skills to be disciplined by an overall concern for what health is, how to promote health. This again is a lifetime project by which a surgeon shapes himself as a subject, and in this way the category of surgeon becomes a subjective category.

The category of psychoanalyst also is essentially subjective. First, the process of internalizing the capacities involved in being a psychoanalyst is essentially incomplete; second, the processes of internalization help to constitute the subjectivity of the psychoanalyst. They shape the kind of subject he is.

To associate to a different realm, consider the thirteen-year-old who, once the ceremony is over, thinks that she is now a Bat Mitzvah. What does she think? There are various things she may think and there are various ways what she thinks might be true. To sharpen the example, let us assume she has learned to read Hebrew, has learned to read from the Torah with skill, and has even begun to pray. Now she may think that, to be a Bat Mitzvah is to be called before the Torah. But what does it mean to be called before the Torah? The proper understanding, I think, is that one has acquired the relevant skills and gone through the appropriate ceremony so that one is in a position to spend a lifetime being called before the Torah. This is not a capacity that is acquired once and for all; rather, it is a lifetime calling ever to shape oneself in relation to a sacred text. In that sense, the process of becoming a Bat Mitzvah is one that never ends—or, should it end, it is the end of oneself as a religious, Jewish person.

Of course, becoming a Bat Mitzvah requires the acquisition of certain skills. She also needed to go through a certain ceremony. These are certain objective facts about her. But their importance lies strictly in the contribution they make to her subjectivity. They put her in a position where there is some meaning in the gesture by which she takes responsibility for being called before the Torah. For that is what she has done at age thirteen: she has taken responsibility for becoming a certain kind of a person. But becoming a certain kind of a person is not itself a process that should come to an end. The process of becoming a certain kind of a person is life itself, and should that becoming come to an end, so does that kind of life.

So, to become a Bat Mitvah in the proper sense is to recognize, however implicitly, that the process of internalization never comes to an end. One is ever in the process of shaping oneself as a subject before the Torah.

The mistaken understanding is to think that once the ceremony is over, the case is settled. One can thereby answer whether one is a Bat Mitzvah or Bar Mitzvah by appealing to the certificate, the rabbi's signature, collective memory, synagogue records, and so on. The question is seen as being settled by certain objective facts: whether a certain ceremony did or did not occur. This is utterly different from the question of whether at that ceremony one genuinely accepted responsibility for be-

coming a certain kind of a subject. The objective understanding will be precisely what occurs in a culture where
organized religion has gone dead, but certain forms remain as moribund shells. At this point the established
rituals—Bar Mitzvah, wedding, funeral—have gone dead
as religious occasions, though they are still needed as
rites of passage. Since one needs to be a Bar Mitzvah or a
Bat Mitzvah to participate in the ceremony, one needs to
be able to say, "Yes, I am a Bat Mitvah," to be able to
participate, say, in a minyan, the quorum of ten adult
Jews that is required before certain prayers can be said.
The fact that it is the objective sense of Bat Mitzvah that
is being deployed serves to cover over the fact that the
subjective sense, along with its concomitant place in religious life, has gone dead.

Now think of the ideas of having a complete analysis or completing one's training as a psychoanalyst. What
could these ideas mean? It seems to me that insofar as
these ideas have legitimacy, they indicate that one is in a
position meaningfully to accept responsibility for living
a certain kind of life with one's unconscious motivations
and with the unconscious motivations of others. In the
case of a complete analysis, it is not that there are no
more conflicts, but that one is in a position to understand actively, in one's living, what those conflicts are.
One is able to take some action with respect to them,
and above all, one is able to avoid being lived by them.
The process of actively and understandingly living with
one's conflicts—of "making the unconscious conscious"—is itself the life of becoming a certain kind of

subject. It is not something one completes once and for all; it is something that is always fresh, always beginning. It is only when one gets trapped by one's conflicts that things get old, that one starts to go dead as a subject.

Similarly, completing one's training as a psychoanalyst means that one has sufficiently grasped one's own unconscious conflicts, has learned sufficiently about psychoanalytic theory and how to apply it that one is finally in a position meaningfully to accept responsibility for helping others to uncover and live with their own unconscious motivations. Completing training, properly understood, signals a new beginning in the process of shaping oneself as a subject, a process that itself has no end. But there is an ever-present danger in professional training that candidates are encouraged to conceive of completing their training along the lines of becoming a barber-surgeon rather than becoming a doctor, or along the lines of the Bat Mitzvah who is done at 13 rather than just beginning.

If a psychoanalyst is never finished internalizing his role as a psychoanalyst, it would seem that some of that unfinished internalization ought to revolve around the concept of internalization itself. *Internalization* is a central concept in psychoanalysis. It is used to designate not only central psychological processes by which the psyche is originally formed in infancy, but also certain crucial aspects of the therapeutic process of psychoanalysis. For the analytic process is thought to consist, at least partially, in a process by which the analysand comes to internalize the capacity for analysis. Analysis is not supposed to be over once analyst and analysand cease meeting; rather, the analysand is supposed to be in a position where she can carry on the activity of analysis largely on her own. But what is this process? How can we think of this process as constituting psychoanalysis?

As it turns out, these are tricky questions. We know from psychoanalysis itself that processes of internalization have significant unconscious dimensions. Indeed, some forms of internalization, such as introjection and identification, are largely or completely unconscious. But even explicit and conscious processes of internalization, say, learning to tie one's shoe, have significant unconscious threads. For example, the anxiety of not knowing, the dependence on one's parents or teachers, the significant erotic and hate-filled relations with those who teach, the unconscious senses of self-worth and of mastery over the world—all these and much more will inevitably get entangled with learning to tie one's shoe. More than likely, they will get reawakened when, later in life, one again tries to acquire a new skill.

Psychoanalysis is supposed to constitute itself around the idea that we avoid all forms of suggestion. But if the psychoanalytic process inevitably involves a process of internalization, and if internalization itself inevitably has a significant unconscious dimension, then doesn't suggestion lie at the heart of the psychoanalytic process after all? If we don't acknowledge this unconscious suggestion, aren't we keeping something unconscious in the name of "making the unconscious conscious"?

It was easy to make fun of the religious figure who was "a little bit stupid," but might we not as psychoanalysts be in the embarrassing position of (unconsciously) suggesting to our patients that there should be no suggestion? Even worse, consider the training of candidates at psychoanalytic institutes. Are our training analysts in effect suggesting to candidates—in training analyses as well as in courses—that they go off and suggest to others that there should be no suggestion? For all of us who have been psychoanalytically trained, the "they" in the last sentence is really "we." How would we know that, unbeknownst to ourselves, we are not responding to the master's suggestion by spreading the word that there should be no suggestion? Of course, trained psychoanalysts are not supposed to have masters, but if we are unconsciously living out the suggestions of others, then we have masters, whether we know it or not. To focus the point even more sharply, how do *I* know that in writing this chapter, and thereby spreading the word that in psychoanalysis there should be no suggestion, how do I know that I am not somehow responding to the suggestions of my psychoanalytic masters? Unbeknownst to myself, might I be as ridiculous a figure as those disciples who spread the master's word that there should be no disciples?

Actually our problem is worse. For if there is a practical contradiction here between the content of what we are saying—there should be no suggestion—and the (suggestive) forms in which we are communicating that message, that contradiction is hidden beneath the surface of our activity. This is quite unlike the religious figure, whose absurdity is patent. If there are suggestive forms within psychoanalysis, they are unconscious, so if there is a practical contradiction embedded in our work, it is not at all easy to see that this is so. Yet, we are the ones who pride ourselves on being able to understand the unconscious; we are the ones who claim that we can live relatively well with our own unconscious and that we can help others with theirs. Does that not make us doubly ridiculous, getting unconsciously entangled in our own unconscious in the name of helping others with theirs?

Talk about possibilities for irony! Consider this possible gap between the aspirations (no suggestion), the pretense (no suggestion), and the reality (laden with suggestion) of being a psychoanalyst. The doctor of the unconscious is busily being "doctored" by his unconscious—and unconsciously "doctoring" the unconscious of others. Why haven't we been more attuned to this looming embarrassment? In part, because it is so much more gratifying to live out this embarrassment rather than notice it. If we (unconsciously) use the positive transference rather than analyze it, we can achieve results that, on the surface at least, look rather decisive. Our patients will tell us they feel increased emotional freedom and marvel at our abilities as analysts. They may even spread the word that in our commitment to freedom, we do not want any quick transference cures. I draw in broad brush-strokes to bring out the farce, but subtle forms of this caricature are not uncommon.

I am not here concerned with diagnosing the various ways in which analysts subvert the analytic process. Rather, I am concerned with the question of whether, even at its best, psychoanalysis embodies a practical contradiction. For if the therapeutic action essentially relies on a process of internalization, and if internalization inevitably has an unconscious dimension, then are we not inevitably relying on the unconscious processes we are supposed to be analyzing?

How painstakingly difficult it is to answer this question! For it is no good simply saying, however sincerely, that psychoanalysis should not rely on suggestion, for that declaration may ultimately be no more than the first step in the absurd two-step by which we suggest there should be no suggestion. As students of the unconscious, we ought to be aware how difficult it is to escape its wiles, not just for our patients but for ourselves. By now, analysts are ready to acknowledge how their own (relatively unconscious) personal feelings—for recognition or for love, their competitiveness, jealousy, etc.—can interact with those of their patients. But we remain relatively unaware of how unconscious motivations can shape the formation of theory and, just as important, the application of theory in a clinical setting. In particular, we continue to assume that whether a theory embodies unconscious forms of suggestion is simply a matter of *what* it says. Thus the difficulty is simply that of making a difficult discovery, perhaps of some hidden content. We remain relatively insensitive to the idea that the hidden suggestion may lie not in *what* the theory says, but in *how* it says it, or, more to the point, in how we appropriate it.

For Loewald, it is the neutrality of the analyst that guarantees that she does not suggest certain outcomes to her patients.[1] But simply insisting on neutrality does not guarantee that it exists. Indeed, affirming our neutrality may be the means by which we hide from ourselves that we are in fact suggesting an outcome. One of the hallmarks of analytic neutrality is, for Loewald, objectivity: "This objectivity cannot mean the avoidance of being available to the patient as an object. The objectivity of the analyst has reference to the patient's transference distortions. Increasingly, through the objective analysis of them, the analyst becomes not only potentially but actually available as a new object, by eliminating step by step impediments represented by these transferences, to a new object-relationship."[2] How are we to understand this claim? Here is one way not to become a "Loewaldian": to use this claim to gratify our own narcissism. We condescend to the previous generation as having misunderstood objectivity—as having used the concept defensively as a way of remaining unavailable to the analysand. Then we assume that objectivity is something we have now achieved in our revised understanding of object relations. Such a position (on its own) can be used to legitimate the most grotesque abuses of psychoanalysis. So now that we recognize that we are living in an intersubjective field,

---

1. Loewald (1960), op. cit., p. 225.
2. Loewald (1960), op. cit., p. 225.

with emotions flowing back and forth, in the name of emotional truth, we should thereby tell our patients how we feel. For, after all, this will be getting to the objective truth of the emotional situation. In myriad ways such as this, analysts disguise from themselves that they are suggesting certain outcomes.[3]

The mistake here seems to lie in the (unconscious?) assumption that we are dealing here with, as it were, an objective conception of objectivity. That is, there is a simple fact of the matter whether one is or is not being objective. The earlier generation made a mistake; now we have learned what the facts of objectivity are. The possibility that one can read the passage in this way is, I think, precisely why Loewald hoped there would never be any Loewaldians, for to proclaim the new truths of objectivity—"We're all object relations theorists now!"—is precisely not to get it, and this, irrespective of the importance of being able to adopt an object relations perspective.

To read this passage aright, one needs to be open to a subjective conception of objectivity. That is, objectivity is itself a goal of subjective striving. One does not achieve

---

3. I have had the opportunity to participate in a continuous case seminar, in which an analyst presents a case that has been stretching out over years. The analyst is someone who believes it to be her responsibility to explain clearly to the analysand how she, the analyst, is feeling in relation to the analysand's remarks and associations. I have noticed that, as the years pass, the analyst is getting much better! She is becoming freer in her associations and much more insightful about what she is really feeling. The analysand, for his part, has remained more or less where he was.

this goal once and for all. Rather, being objective as an analyst is in part constituted by the recognition that one is ever in the process of trying to become objective. In part, this requires a perpetual encounter with one's own unconscious motivations; in part, it requires a living engagement with the question of whether there might not be hidden forms of suggestion in a therapy that itself is supposed to abjure it. In short, the current inquiry is itself part of the continuous activity of becoming objective.

It helps to be attuned to irony. Loewald's strategy, as we have seen, is the sympathetic subversion of a *pretense*: that objectivity requires a certain kind of detachment—namely, one in which we avoid being available to our patients. But he does not then simply flip over to the other side and say that therefore we should be subjective, or therefore we should be intersubjective. Rather, he holds onto an *aspiration*: that analysis does require objectivity, but of a different sort. But whatever this objectivity is, it must be a way in which we make ourselves available to our patients; thus, it must be a way in which we shape ourselves as subjects. At this point we can become intersubjectivists if we want, or object relations theorists. But if we want to remain analysts, we must come to understand what it is to be objective within this intersubjective setting. To grasp this as an essentially subjective question is to recognize that it is a question that goes on without end. Thus the passage quoted above is not, I think, something one can come to understand once and for all. One begins to understand it when one reads it as setting a lifetime task for understanding.

Following Freud, Loewald turns to art to capture
the psychoanalytic situation. The idea that the analyst is
only a mirror that reflects back the patient's transferences
is, Loewald says, "only a half-truth":

> The analyst in actuality does not only reflect the trans-
> ference distortions. In his interpretations he implies
> aspects of undistorted reality which the patient begins
> to grasp step by step as transferences are interpreted.
> This undistorted reality is mediated to the patient by
> the analyst, mostly by the process of chiseling away the
> transference distortions, or, as Freud has beautifully
> put it, using an expression of Leonardo da Vinci, *per
> via di levare* as in sculpting, not *per via di porre* as in
> painting. In sculpturing, the figure to be created comes
> into being by taking away from the material; in paint-
> ing, by adding something to the canvas. In analysis, we
> bring out the true form by taking away the neurotic
> distortions. However, as in sculpture, we must have, if
> only in rudiments, an image of that which needs to be
> brought into its own. The patient, by revealing himself
> to the analyst, provides rudiments of such an image
> through all the distortions—an image that the analyst
> has to focus in his mind, thus holding it in safe keep-
> ing for the patient to whom it is mainly lost. It is this
> tenuous reciprocal tie which represents the germ of a
> new object-relationship.[4]

---

4. Loewald (1960), op. cit., pp. 225–226.

It is easy enough to see how this passage could be invoked to legitimate suggesting an outcome to the analysand: "I am 'holding on' to an image of who you really are, and in various ways I encourage you to adopt it." The interesting task—the subjective task of a psychoanalyst—is to grasp how not to understand the passage in this way. If the distinction between painting and sculpture is going to be a distinction that makes a difference, it cannot be that in painting one lays on a preordained image, whereas in sculpting one chisels away until one reaches it. For in both of these cases, the artist is imposing an image onto matter. For the distinction to make the right kind of difference, we need to give some content to the idea that in sculpting we are merely washing away (*levare*) neurotic accretions. How do we give content to this kind of taking away?

Consider, for purposes of comparison, another account of taking away. In a footnote in *Concluding Unscientific Postscript*, Climacus says that his "book is written for informed readers whose misfortune is that they know too much":

> Because everybody knows it, the Christian truth has gradually become a triviality, of which it is difficult to secure a primitive impression. This being the case, the art of *communication* at last becomes the art of *taking away*, of luring something away from someone. This seems very strange and ironical, and yet I believe that I have succeeded in expressing precisely what I mean. When a man has his mouth so full that he is prevented

from eating, does giving him food consist in stuffing
still more of it into his mouth, or does it consist in taking some of it away so that he can begin to eat?[5]

Here is an ironical picture of feeding a man by taking
food away from him. For his mouth is so stuffed that
what is in it can no longer function as food. When
Climacus says he writes for those who "know too much,"
the irony is evident. In all their knowledge, they do not
know; they do not even know that they don't know. It is
through their "knowledge" that the "Christian truth"
has become a triviality. The answer to this cannot be to
take away certain facts—only to replace them with others. We take away from them the idea that being Christian essentially involves being born of Christian parents,
of being baptized in a Christian church, and so on. But
if in this process of taking away we hold onto the "rudiments, an image of that which needs to be brought into
its own," this cannot mean that there is one more objective fact—say, getting circumcised—and if only you
take care of that you will finally be a Christian. No, the
rudiments, the image we have to hold onto is the idea
that in the process of taking away, the person will be
able to transform himself as a subject. He comes to see
that these are not the kind of differences that could
make a difference, and he starts to search for the kind
of difference that could. That is, we are trying to facili-

---

5. Kierkegaard (1846), op. cit., p. 245n.

tate a process that makes a subjective, not an objective, difference.

In analysis, it is tempting to say that we are taking food out of a stuffed mouth in order that the subject should at last be able to speak. However, that suggests that, but for a stuffed mouth, the subject is capable of speaking. The beauty of using an example from sculpture is that it remains systematically vague how much of the subject is already there.

Freud himself was fond of using an archaeological metaphor to describe the psychoanalytic process: it was as though the analyst came upon some shards, and began a dig.[6] But even if we can imagine an archaeological excavation in which one simply washed away the accretions of sand and mud, we would be simply uncovering fully formed artifacts that were there anyway, independently of the excavation. But if we think of the psyche as itself a psychological achievement, then we ought to be able to conceive of the psychoanalytic process not simply as the discovery of an independently existing reality, but as a process by which the psyche comes into its own. These are the "rudiments, an image of that which needs to be brought into its own"; it is not any particular objective image of what this person might become, but rather a subjective image of this person becoming a person.

Michaelangelo said that he could see the *Pieta* in the stone. On a contemporary understanding of those words, this cannot be the right use of a sculpting meta-

---

6. See, for example, Freud (1896, p. 192).

phor for psychoanalysis. For, we want to say, Michael-angelo had an image in his mind of the *Pieta,* and what he "saw" was a way to realize it in stone. But can we, for a moment, loosen our contemporary assumptions about the process of artistic production? Michaelangelo lived in a religious age, and his art was an expression of his religiosity. Perhaps this has become impossible to grasp in a secular age, but I invite you to imagine that what Michaelangelo "saw" was not so much a physical image as divine subjectivity finding some kind of physical real-ization. What he saw was not an object, but a subject com-ing into being.

For Loewald, it is *the patient* who provides the rudi-ments, the image, of what needs to be brought into its own. That is, the patient provides his own rudiments of what he is to become. The analyst merely holds it in safe-keeping, for the patient "to whom it is mainly lost." Of course, these words can be invoked defensively to cover over the projections of the analyst: "I'm not projecting, I see his true core." One is tempted to say, "When one hears those words, duck!" And yet, just because a form of words can be used to promote self-delusions, it does not follow that the very same words cannot also be used to say something true. The problem lies not in the words themselves, but in the life one is living with them.

Unfortunately, contemporary psychotherapeutic culture encourages a professional life in which Loewald's words will tend to be misappropriated. For there is a wide-spread assumption, expressed at various levels of sophis-tication, that psychoanalysis and psychotherapy are essentially corrective emotional experiences. There are, of course, many caricatured versions, but let's take a serious model of therapeutic action: On one preeminent paradigm, the analyst offers up a benign and analytically minded superego for the analysand to internalize.[7] Gradually, the analysand projects primitive superego functions onto the analyst, the analyst interprets transferences distortions, and the analysand gradually internalizes a benign, analytic superego—like that of the analyst. If this is the truth of psychoanalysis, then, as Paul Gray has pointed out, it is still based on hypnotic forms of suggestion. There may be gradual increments—of introjection, incorporation, internalization—by which a primitive superego is replaced by the image of the analyst, but it is essentially the same suggestive process. Gray concedes that therapeutic action by means of this kind of internalization can occur in many valuable analyses; the problem, for him, is to assume that this is the ultimate therapeutic factor for all analyses.[8] For that is, first, to concede that the therapeutic action of psychoanalysis essentially rests upon suggestion. Thus it is to concede that the analysis is essentially entangled in practical contradiction: suggesting that there should be no suggestion. Second, it inhibits the development of techniques that genuinely promote autonomy.

---

7. Strachey (1934). This article has provoked a long line of successor articles.
8. Gray (1982).

It seems to me that Loewald escapes this criticism, but it is not easy to see how. The best way is to work through the temptation to see Loewald as promoting an internalization model of this type. Loewald does see the parent–child relationship as providing the archaic paradigm for the analytic relationship:

> The parent–child relationship can serve as a model here. The parent ideally is in an empathic relationship of understanding the child's particular stage of development, yet ahead in his vision of the child's future and mediating this vision to the child in his dealing with him. This vision, informed by the parent's own experience and knowledge of growth and future, is, ideally, a more articulate and more integrated version of *the core of being* that the child presents to the parent. The "more" that the parent sees and knows, he mediates to the child so that the child in identification with it can grow. The child, by internalizing aspects of the parent, also internalizes the parent's image of the child—an image that is mediated to the child in the thousand different ways of being handled, bodily and emotionally. Early identification as part of ego development, built up through introjection of maternal aspects, includes introjection of the mother's image of the child. Part of what is introjected is the image of the child as seen, felt, smelled, heard, touched by the mother. It would perhaps be more correct to add that what happens is not wholly a process of introjection, if introjection is used as a term for intrapsychic activity. The bodily handling of and concern with

the child, the manner in which the child is fed, touched, cleaned, the way it is looked at, talked to, called by name, recognized and re-recognized—all these and many other ways of communicating with the child, and communicating to him his identity, sameness, unity and individuality, shape and mould him so that he can begin to identify himself, to feel and recognize himself as one and as separate from others yet with others. The child begins to experience himself as a centered unity by being centered upon.

In analysis, if it is to be a process leading to structural changes, interactions of a comparable nature have to take place.[9]

To understand this passage, everything hangs on how one understands the claim that interactions of a *comparable nature* have to take place. If one assumes that one already understands how the analytic situation is like the parental paradigm, then one will use a statement like this simply to legitimate one's current point of view. So, for instance, imagine a therapist who thinks she should be a benign, supportive figure for her patients, sometimes giving good advice, encouraging their self-esteem, and so on. She may think she is providing a mothering function that the patient did not adequately receive in childhood. Thus she is going on in a mothering way, while correcting for the mothering deficits of childhood. If

---

9. Loewald (1960), op. cit., pp. 229–230.

such a therapist reads this passage, *and assumes that she already knows what kinds of interactions are of comparable nature*, she will assume it supports her therapeutic stance. In this way she locks herself into an automatic sense of what it is to go on in a similar way. This is (automatic) repetition on the part of the analyst.

The mistake here is to assume that there is a fixed content to the comparison between the mother–child and the analyst–analysand interactions. Rather one should recognize that it is in the nature of a comparison that one can put it to all kinds of uses. The right kinds of comparisons can only be made within the context of one's own attempts to shape oneself as a psychoanalyst. There is no fixed content to the comparison that exists independently of the attempt to deepen oneself as an analyst. It seems to me that the right way to read the phrase "interactions of a comparable nature have to take place" is with surprise, a dash of incredulity, and some intellectual delight. Rather than assume we already know what is meant, we should think, "Given that the parent–child relation is so full of teaching, positive direction, and prohibition, so chocked full of unconscious suggestions of who to be and how to go on, and given that we assume that the analytic relationship should abjure all of that, how, in heaven's name, can the analytic relationship be anything like that?!" Rather than simply acquiescing to the parental model, as though we already knew what that was, we should see it as posing an incredibly challenging puzzle. In trying

to come to serious grips with that puzzle, we deepen
ourselves as analysts. Thus the idea of "interactions of a
comparable nature" should be read as an essentially subjective category. We find out what we mean by this as we
deepen ourselves as analysts.

Let's sharpen the problem. Here is how Loewald
describes the dynamics of interaction in early stages of
development:

> The mother recognizes and fulfils the needs of the in-
> fant. Both recognition and fulfillment of a need are at
> first beyond the ability of the infant, not merely the
> fulfillment. The understanding recognition of the
> infant's need on the part of the mother represents a
> gathering together of as yet undifferentiated urges of
> the infant, urges that in the acts of recognition and
> fulfillment by the mother undergo a first organi-
> zation into some kind of directed drive. . . . Gradually,
> both recognition and satisfaction of the need come
> within the grasp of the growing infant itself. . . . The
> whole complex dynamic constellation is one of mutual
> responsiveness where nothing is introjected by the
> infant that is not brought to it by the mother, *although
> brought by her often unconsciously.* And a prerequisite for
> introjection and identification is the gathering media-
> tion of structure and direction by the mother in her
> caring activities. As the mediating environment
> conveys structure and direction to the unfolding psy-
> chophysical entity, the environment begins to gain

structure and direction in the experience of that entity.[10]

It is easy enough to put these two just-quoted passages together to justify a touchy-feely approach to psychoanalysis. The analyst can then see herself as providing a better parental experience than the patient had the first time around. It would even seem to be all right to let the patient unconsciously internalize aspects of the analyst, just as he earlier did with his mother, as part of the analytic process. If a Loewaldian is someone who justifies *this* stance in his name, no wonder Loewald hoped there would never be any! But how does he escape this fate? Or, rather, how might we read him otherwise?

The key is to read these passages in context. In particular, one should keep an eye on the quartet *neutrality, objectivity, love,* and *respect.*

The analyst, through objective interpretation of transference distortions, increasingly becomes available to the patient as a new object. And this not primarily in the sense of an object not previously met, but the newness consists in the patient's rediscovery of the early paths

10. Loewald (1960), op. cit., pp. 237–238; my emphasis. I am going to assume that by "mother," Loewald means not only the biological mother but any parenting figures—the nurturing environment—who through there mutual responsiveness provide material for introjection for the infant.

of the development of object-relations leading to a new way of relating to objects and of being oneself. *Through all the transference distortions the patient reveals rudiments at least of the core of himself* and "objects" that have been distorted. It is this core, rudimentary and vague as it may be, to which the analyst has reference when he interprets transferences and defenses, and not some abstract concept of reality or normality, if he is to reach the patient. *If the analyst keeps his central focus on this emerging core he avoids moulding the patient in the analyst's own image or imposing on the patient his own concept of what the patient should become. It requires objectivity and neutrality the essence of which is love and respect for the individual and for individual development.*[11]

Obviously, it is possible for an analyst to use a passage like this to gratify his own narcissism. This would occur if he assumed he already knew what it was to love or care about his patient. Satisfied that he cared, he would then think that he could see his patient's emerging core. This is the route to projection and suggestion in the name of therapy. Instead, one needs to see the link between love, on the one hand, and objectivity and neutrality, on the other, as incredibly problematic and thought provoking. Rather than assuming that because one does care for one's patients in a benign and relatively open way that therefore one is dealing with them in an objective and neutral way, one should allow the puzzling demands of

---

11. Loewald (1960), op. cit., pp. 228–229; my emphasis.

objectivity and neutrality to sink in. One can then ask oneself the question—as a real, practical question—of whether one's care for the patient, no matter how benign, well meaning, and undirected, is in fact the right kind of care for the therapeutic process. This is the kind of question that itself has no end.

The analyst in his interpretations brings the analysand back to the core of himself. It is easy enough to abuse this claim. The analyst in his grandiosity has a better idea than the analysand of who the analysand essentially is, and then by explicit means and unconscious suggestion he lets the analysand know who he should become. The analysand, in an unanalyzed positive transference, then internalizes this image of himself; a false self is created, and analyst and analysand congratulate themselves on a job well done!

One needs a completely different sense of bringing an analysand back to his core. In particular, one needs to think of the idea of a core, without that core having any determinate content. To this end, consider what all forms of neurosis have in common: the various structures of the psyche are split off from each other and set against each other in various forms of conflict. The forms of conflict may differ, but separation of the psyche into conflicting parts is the essence of neurosis. But then there is a perfectly good sense in saying that the neurotic doesn't have a core: his psyche is split into parts that are themselves at war with each other. Of course, a person may have all sorts of determinate content in his psyche: from an ego position, he may tell us who he thinks he really is;

from a superego position, he may tell us what he'd like to be; and when he acts out he may express all sorts of id-like wishes that come from deep within him. Yet it is a mistake to assume that any of these contents reveal his core, for he is such a self-embattled person that a core is what he's missing. His ego-claims to identity are themselves a defensive reaction, both against a punishing superego and the onslaught of id-wishes he can barely keep under control. Similarly, for each of the parts in relation to the others.

I've overstated the case to make a point: the core is not any determinate content in the psyche, nor is it any one of the psychic parts as opposed to the others. Rather, *the core is the elementary capacity of the psyche to hold itself together.* It is this capacity that exists only in "rudiments" in the neurotic patient. And it is this image—not any determinate content, but the idea that one can hold oneself together—that the analyst has to hold "in safe keeping for the patient to whom it is mainly lost."

Perhaps now is the time to note that the neurotic psyche is ripe for irony.[12] For the possibility of irony opens up in the gap between aspiration, pretense, and reality, but that gap will always be there in neurotic conflict. There are myriad ways this gap can open up, but let me give a few schematic illustrations. One can think of id-like wishes as archaic voices of aspiration. They are trying to get themselves satisfied. Over against this, the

---

12. Actually, this is the key to Woody Allen's jokes: to make this irony explicit and to present it in an exaggerated form.

neurotic ego is a voice of pretense. It tries to pretend either that these id-like wishes don't exist (repression) or that they are being gratified in some ego-acceptable way. Obviously, from the viewpoint of the id, the ego's claim that wishes are being gratified is ridiculous.

A punishing superego, for its part, can be thought of as an utterly unironic critique of the pretenses of the ego. The superego is itself a form of aspiration: it upholds certain ideals. Ironically, it is often formed by putting a NOT! in front of the id's aspirations. In its cruel form it is also a devastating criticism of the ego's falling short. One might say that precisely because a capacity for irony is missing that what emerges in its place is a neurotic sense of guilt.

A psychoanalytic interpretation exploits this possibility for irony; it tries to bring aspiration and pretense together. That is, the interpretation tries to bring to light how the pretenses of the ego do or do not fit with the aspirations of the id and superego. In this sense the analyst is not teaching any doctrine or trying to impart any particular idea. Rather, the interpretation facilitates a process by which the analysand comes back to himself. That is, it brings different aspects of himself into some form of communication (however rudimentary). Properly understood, psychoanalytic interpretation is a form of irony. And in working through irony, structural change becomes possible. This takes some explanation.

Loewald does not mention irony explicitly, but it is there in his account of interpretation:

An interpretation can be said to comprise two elements,
inseparable from each other. The interpretation takes
with the patient the step towards true regression, as
against the neurotic compromise formation, thus
clarifying for the patient his true regression level [id-
aspirations], which has been covered and made unrecognizable by defensive operations and structures.
Secondly, by this very step it mediates to the patient the
higher integrative level to be reached. [I.e., it opens up
a nonpretentious understanding.] The interpretation
thus creates the possibility for freer interplay between
the unconscious and preconscious systems, whereby the
preconscious regains its originality and intensity, lost to
the unconscious in repression, and the unconscious regains access to and capacity for progression in the direction of higher organization. . . . This process may be seen
as the internalized version of the overcoming of a differential in the *interaction process* described above as integrative experience. Internalization itself is dependent on
interaction and is made possible again in the analytic process. The analytic process then consists in certain integrative experiences between patient and analyst as the
foundation for the internalized version of such experiences: reorganization of the ego, "structural change."[13]

Let's get clear on what is meant by the interaction process between analyst and analysand, for this is the process that leads to internalization. For Loewald, there is a

---

13. Loewald (1960), op. cit., pp. 240–241.

differential in psychic organization between analyst and analysand, and it is this differential that provides the opportunity for psychic growth.[14] But when Loewald says that the analyst has a higher level of psychic organization, this does not mean that he possesses some special knowledge that the analysand lacks. In particular, it cannot mean that the analyst possesses the secret of the analysand's identity, and that analysis consists somehow in passing that knowledge along. Analysis is not an unconscious version of "Father Knows Best." Nor does higher psychic organization mean a rigid structure that simply has greater complexity. As Loewald repeatedly stresses, higher organization consists in part in the capacity to regress, to play, to make loose associations—ironically, to give up structure. What higher organization does require is that when one does give up structure, one has not thereby lost it. One retains the capacity to come back. This higher psychical organization needs to be understood in terms of its dynamism and flexibility, its capacity for poetic movements, not in terms of some fixed structure. And analysis needs to be understood as enhancing this capacity, which, among other things, is a capacity for irony.

Let me explain what I mean via a clinical vignette.[15] This example is fascinating not only because it beautifully displays the irony appropriate to psychoanalytic interpretation, but also because the author takes him-

---

14. Loewald (1960), op. cit., pp. 238–240.
15. I take this from Lawrence Levenson's (1998) brilliant paper.

self to be making an anti-Loewaldian point. As we shall see, the example is anti-Loewaldian in the sense that Loewald didn't want there to be any Loewaldians. In fact, it is an excellent example of the process of internalization that Loewald is talking about.

Dr. L. is a gifted analyst who is concerned about theories of therapeutic action that depend on the internalization of the analyst as a superego figure.[16] The danger is this: if the analyst believes that therapeutic action occurs through the internalization of the analyst as a new superego, then he will have a tendency to allow certain defensive functions to go unanalyzed. After all, the superego is a defensive structure. Originally it was a compromise formation that emerged out of the conflicts of the oedipal period. The child is conflicted between love and hate toward his parents, and through internalization he turns some of his aggression on himself as a way of controlling his own aggressive impulses. Is this essentially defensive solution just going to be repeated in the analytic situation, albeit at a higher level of sophistication? The problem Dr. L. sees is that even if this harsh superego is ameliorated, if the analyst's therapeutic goal is to allow for the internalization of a more benign superego, there may nevertheless be defensive functions that get overlooked. Are we not thereby shortchanging our analysands? And, to put it in the context of our current inquiry, are we not facilitating the creation of a certain

---

16. Levenson is influenced by the writings on technique of Paul Gray (see Gray, 1994).

kind of defense precisely as we declare that the analysand
has been freed of his defenses?

> Dr. L. is working in the termination phase with
> Mr. A., a middle-aged unmarried professional who
> "entered analysis because of anxiety, social inhibi-
> tions, and a view of himself as 'wearing a nice mask
> to hide the real, ugly, nasty me.'"[17] Mr. A. had diffi-
> culty with his aggressive impulses, particularly with
> those directed toward people in authority, and this
> soon became prominent in the transference. He ex-
> perienced Dr. L. as a restraining, controlling author-
> ity. Over the course of the analysis, Mr. A. was able
> to analyze his central neurotic conflicts, and overall
> had a successful analysis. But we focus now on a few
> moments in the termination phase.

In the fourth year of analysis, Mr. A. began to talk
more frequently about terminating the analysis, but he
always talked of "quitting" it rather than, say, ending or
finishing it. When asked, Mr. A. said that quitting felt
strong, masculine, and decisive, his decision rather than
Dr. L.'s, and it was far preferable to taking the end of the
analysis "lying down." He associated to various times in
his adolescence when he asserted his independence from

---

17. Levenson (1998), op. cit., p. 855. I am going to give a bare
outline of this clinical case in order to bring one moment into
focus. Readers who are interested in more detail are urged to consult this article.

his father through acts of defiance and rebellion. He then added that rebelling is not the same as becoming truly independent. Talk of "quitting" seemed to him to indicate that he was ending the analysis in a rebellion.

In the ensuing months, Mr. A. began to "warn" Dr. L. that he was soon going to ask to set a date for termination. In reflecting on this, Mr. A. said that discussing termination felt like an aggressive act, for it felt like acting rather than analyzing. Now that he thought about it, he used the activity of analyzing as itself a means of keeping himself in bounds. It felt dangerous and aggressive to break open this way he had of controlling himself.

When he finally did bring up termination, Mr. A. first felt joy, but then felt hurt, angry, rejected, and abandoned when Dr. L. agreed to set a date. It was as though the roles had suddenly switched, and Dr. L. was now experienced as the aggressor, the person who was rejecting and abandoning him. A few weeks later, Mr. A. asked Dr. L. whether there were any guidelines about when he could call him, should any difficulties arise after termination. Dr. L. responded that Mr. A. didn't seem to trust his own judgment, and was turning to him as an authority figure.

About three months before termination, Mr. A. began to speak of all the gains he had made in analysis. He wanted Dr. L. to know how much happier, freer, and more relaxed he felt. He was pleased with all the life changes he had been able to make: getting married, buying a house, having a child. He knew that these external changes were a manifestation of significant internal changes. He expressed in a heartfelt way that he hoped Dr. L. understood how much this had meant to him. These remarks fit Dr. L.'s own sense that it had been a far-reaching and successful analysis. "On the surface, at least, it seemed that this taking stock of what had been accomplished in his analysis was part of a 'rebuilding' or synthesizing process appropriate to termination."[18]

But then there was this cough. It began with a respiratory infection but it lingered on, and it would emerge in a session when Mr. A. would start talking about hostile feelings. Was the cough a symptom of an underlying psychic conflict, covered over by all the sincerely meant testimonials? Mr. A., by now an experienced analysand, himself began to wonder about the meaning of his cough.

> [He] did not recognize their connection to hostile wishes until an extended fit of coughing occurred when he suddenly became intensely angry with me, saying, "Do I want to tell you to fuck off!" He then began coughing uncontrollably for several minutes, finally leaving the office for a minute to go to the bathroom for a drink of water. Returning to the couch, he asked, "Why would I want to tell you to fuck off? You haven't done anything but been here."
>
> I said, "Maybe that's why."

---

18. Levenson (1998), op. cit., p. 858.

"Yes, you're the doctor," he replied. "Why haven't you cured me? I've been waiting for you to fix me."

This was the moment when Mr. A. experienced the full intensity of his hostility toward me in the waning months of the analysis.[19]

In the context of this analysis, that simple remark—"Maybe that's why"—is a perfect interpretation. It refers Mr. A. back to his own just-uttered and sincerely felt words, and it *offers him* an invitation to bring out the irony. When Mr. A. said, "You haven't done anything but been here," he meant it as a compliment. He was trying to say, "I've got no grounds for complaint; you've always been there for me." This is the voice of pretense, the voice of the ego. Dr. L.'s simple interpretation turns this meaning on its head. It brings to Mr. A.'s attention that the very same words, the ones he has just uttered so sincerely, can also be the voice of complaint, "You haven't done *anything* but been here!" In effect, Dr. L.'s interpretation highlights the voice of aspiration, and therefore of complaint: "I'm still full of wishes for a special relationship with you, one in which you effect a magical cure, and all you've ever done is sit there!"

By referring him back to his own words, Dr. L. puts Mr. A. in a position where he can see for himself the distance between his pretense and his aspirations. He can now see that while he would like to be a grateful and

19. Levenson (1998), op. cit., p. 858.

successful analysand, and to some extent he is, he would also like that to be the whole truth, and that it is not. He is also angry and disappointed that his wishes have not been gratified. There are things he wanted he did not get, the analysis is about to be over, it's clear now he'll never get it, and he's angry about that, though he is unconscious of his anger, just as he is unconscious of his wishes. But what is more striking is that the very words that he uses to express his gratitude are used by him dynamically to cover over his anger, an anger that would be expressed with the very same words!

Here one can see quite clearly that it is constitutional of Mr. A.'s neurosis that he cannot see the irony of his own words. For if the words "You haven't done anything but been here" are going to serve to express his gratitude and cover over his anger, then it is crucial that he not see that his words might also be used to express his anger. As soon as Mr. A. begins to grasp that "You haven't done anything but been here" might also be used by him to express his anger, then those words start to lose their ability to cover up the anger. This is what it is for the analysand to begin to appreciate the irony of his own remarks.

The analyst said simply, "Maybe that's why." It is crucial that one understands this remark as completely earnest, just as we see it bring out the irony. By "maybe" the analyst means *maybe*. It is simply a mistake to assume that an ironic remark cannot also be earnest. It is a travesty of the concept of irony—a true confusion—facilitated by bad dictionary definitions that irony is simulated or feigned ignorance. But the analyst genuinely does not know. At most he can issue an invitation to the analysand to explore for himself this potential gap between pretense and aspiration. It is a distorting fantasy (which itself needs to be analyzed) that the analyst is sitting there with the secret to the analysand's life, and he's going to use cutesy or oracular remarks to make the analysand guess what it is. The analyst says "maybe" because he genuinely does not know. There is no piece of information he is keeping hidden for the analysand to guess. If there is any secret to be elicited, it must be the analysand who tells them both what it is. The most the analyst can do is facilitate the process. He does this by bringing out the irony.

Loewald says, "If an interpretation of unconscious meaning is timely, the words by which this meaning is expressed are recognizable to the patient as expressions of what he experiences."[20] That is, the aspirations are getting expressed as aspirations, and not getting covered over by a distorting pretense. Mr. A. can now feel "You haven't done anything but been here!" as a complaint, not just as a compliment. In so doing he can begin to feel that both the complaint and the compliment are different aspects of himself. In short, in feeling the gap between pretense and aspiration, he also begins to bridge that gap. He begins to bring these conflicting emotions together in a more unified psychical organization.

In this sense, to say that the analyst is at a higher level of psychic organization than the analysand is not

---

20. Loewald (1960), op. cit., p. 238.

self-glorification on the part of the analyst. Nor is it a dogmatic assertion of superiority. Rather, it describes an essential truth of the analytic situation. By the very fact that the neurotic patient is neurotic, he reveals that, in an important sense, he lacks the capacity for irony. To maintain himself in a neurotic position, Mr. A. has to hear "You've done nothing but been here" only as the voice of pretense. It is by developing a capacity for irony that Mr. A. can start to bring the disparate and conflicting parts of himself together. The development of the capacity for irony facilitates psychic organization. Of its essence it serves to organize the psyche by bringing psychic aspirations and psychic pretenses into communication with each other. So precisely in virtue of the fact that the analyst has the capacity for irony and the analysand necessarily lacks it, the psychoanalyst is at a higher level of psychic organization than the analysand. This is not an empirical generalization. There may be all sorts of pathetic cases in which a disorganized analyst approaches a more organized patient. But then it is time for irony about this analytic situation as a whole: what we have in this case is merely the pretense of analysis. For the differential from higher psychical organization (in the analyst) to lower psychical organization (in the analysand) is definitional of the analytic situation.

Dr. L.'s interpretation followed by Mr. A.'s uptake is, I think, precisely what Loewald means by a differential in the interaction process between analyst and analysand leading to internalization. Dr. L. is not communicating any superior or esoteric knowledge about Mr. A.'s true core. Nor is Dr. L. offering himself as an example of a benign superego figure for internalization. Nevertheless, Dr. L. does have a capacity for psychic organization that still exists in only a rudimentary form in Mr. A. It is the capacity to say simply, "Maybe that's why" and invite Mr. A. to look at the disparate meanings of his own words.

If this is the proper form of interaction between analyst and analysand, then the internalization based on it can have nothing essentially to do with the internalization of a benign superego figure. What is essentially internalized in the psychoanalytic process is the appropriate capacity for irony, and this capacity is not located in any particular psychic agency. Rather, it is a capacity to integrate all those agencies via a perpetual process of giving words to aspirations and exposing pretenses for what they are. What is internalized is the capacity for integrating the psyche. This isn't the importation of yet another psychic agency, though it does lead to structural modifications in how all psychic structures relate to each other and thus to structural modifications in the psyche as a whole. Thus the most important use of the concept of internalization is essentially subjective; indeed, it names the process by which a subject becomes *the* subject.

Paul Gray is concerned that in the *name* of internalization an analyst may overlook just such valuable opportunities *for* internalization. That is, if one thinks that the internalization of a benign, analytic superego is itself an essential ingredient in the therapeutic process, one might be tempted not to analyze benign, analytically minded superego transferences. This, an analyst might well think, is preliminary to internalization of such a superego figure. So, if Dr. L. had been under the influence of such a theory of therapeutic action, he might have been tempted to leave the heartfelt thanks unanalyzed. As Gray points out, such thanks are certainly gratifying for the analyst. So much the better if one can leave those remarks at their unexamined surface meaning. The analyst can then help himself to endure the separation by fantasizing that this benign presence will be internalized by the analysand. The analysand will then carry the beloved analyst around with him forever—at least, so the analyst fantasizes.

But if Dr. L. had allowed the heartfelt thanks to pass unnoticed (that is, unnoticed from the point of view of analytic skepticism), he would have left Mr. A. with an unconscious superego defense. He would not have come to see that in his cough he was literally choking with anger. Not only would he be unaware of his angry feelings, but even more importantly, he would have remained unaware of how he used heartfelt thanks as a way of defending against (unconscious) hostile feelings. This sacrifice of a potential psychoanalytic gain could well have flowed from the analyst's holding onto a theory of therapeutic action that calls for the internalization of a superego figure.

All of this is correct and important. It constitutes a serious objection to any theory of therapeutic action that relies on the unconscious internalization of the analyst as a benign superego figure. The danger is that, having recognized this important truth, one then flips too far in the other direction and assumes that therefore unconscious internalizations should be no part of the analytic process. Here one needs to make a distinction between what is *essential* to the therapeutic process and what is likely to be an *inevitable concomitant.* As Gray says, "Although some patients, pathologically and defensively, react more than others to the analyst with incorporations, *probably all show some regressive tendency* in that direction."[21] Levenson adds, "Since internalization of a more benign authority is, as Gray has pointed out, universal and often effective in providing relief of suffering, *it is probably inevitable in all analyses to some degree* even in the termination period."[22] This means that while one needs to banish such primitive internalizations from a proper account of what one relies on in the therapeutic *action* of psychoanalysis, one needs to include them in account of the inevitable occurrences within the therapeutic *process.*[23]

---

21. Gray (1982), op. cit., p. 53; my emphasis. Gray also says, "I would not dispute that suggestive influence may be to some degree *inevitable in any human interaction,* but I am referring to dependence on it and a fostering of it in the analytic situation" (p. 39).
22. Levenson (1998), op. cit., p. 850; my emphasis.
23. In particular, it is a fantasy to assume that just because one is following the techniques of Gray, that therefore no internalization processes are going on. It is one thing to avoid relying on hidden processes of introjection and internalization; it is quite another to think that they therefore don't occur. The former is prudent technique, the latter is wishful thinking. It is similarly wishful to think that these processes don't occur if one adopts a vocabulary to describe therapeutic action that avoids the word *internalization.*

One needs to account for the fact that while superego internalizations may well occur at various levels of sophistication and primitiveness, even in the termination phase of the analysis, one is also fostering the internalization of a capacity for analyzing these unconscious forms of internalization.[24] For it is unrealistic, not to say inhuman, to expect an analyzed person to abjure all unconscious forms of assimilation. Rather, the point is that to the extent that a person does unconsciously internalize various aspirations and pretenses, as he does when he internalizes the analyst as a benign superego figure, he has also the capacity to bring those internalizations to light. It is only the internalization of this latter capacity that properly constitutes the therapeutic action of psychoanalysis.

---

24. See "Comments on Some Instinctual Manifestations of Superego Formation," in Loewald (2000), op. cit., pp. 326–341.

4

Love as a Drive

As you opened a new book, have you ever imagined it was like getting on a train? You don't really know where you are going, there is the allure of adventure, the promise that you are going to be taken someplace new. As the train pulls out of the station, new vistas start to open up, but somewhere along the route things start to get ugly, you want to stop the train. "Do I really have to go *there*?!" It's like a dream turned bad.

That is how I feel when I read Lacan. He begins with an insight he gets from Heidegger—that the human psyche is essentially open to the world. This insight governs his reading of Freud; rather than see the psyche as a closed system upon which a hostile world impinges, Lacan sees it as essentially formed by (and existing in) its engagements in the world. There are astonishing insights along the way; in particular, Lacan has made brilliant use of the idea that precisely because we are so world-directed, it is in our nature to latch onto utterances, sights, and objects, and take them as having significance, though we do not (yet) know what their significance is. We have an oracular sense that it is meant for us, yet we do not understand its meaning.

But though we start from an engagement with the world, we quickly end up disorganized. This is because, for Lacan, the world is an occasion for us to become misled about ourselves. In his famous essay on the mirror stage, the ego is formed on the basis of misperception and misunderstanding.[1] From a psychological point of view, the human infant is born prematurely, thrown into a world that he does not yet have the capacity to inhabit. In particular, his ability to identify with visual images far outstrips his inner reality. Thus, as he sees an image of himself in the mirror, at around six months of age, he will see much more unity in that image than he has internally in fragmented bodily experiences. Lacan also uses the mirror as a metaphor for the mirroring functions of the mother: as the mother gazes on her child, she is projecting unconscious fantasies of who he is that not only far outstrip but also distort the child's living psychic reality. In particular, the mother sees the child as more unified than he is. But the child identifies with that unified image, and thus begins to establish a self-alienated ego. This alienation—using the world as an opportunity to attribute more unity to ourselves than we in fact

---

1. Significantly, translators of Lacan into English like to leave the French word *méconnaissance* untranslated.

have—re-occurs at various stages of organization and development.

On this conception, unification is essentially a form of falsehood—of covering over a truer, underlying disorganization and emptiness. Thus Lacanian psychoanalysis must valorize a process in which this false unity is exposed and undone. It is by now a commonplace of psychoanalysis that there are personalities that present a false unity. There is the false self, the as-if personality, and, of course, Dr. Schreber's "fleetingly improvised person." We all know people who we recognize as being a shell of a human being. Equally obviously, psychoanalysis is formed around the treatment of such people. Even with more richly formed human beings, psychoanalysis focuses in on the false unities that misshape their souls. But Lacan's claim is more radical than that. His claim is that it is *essential* to the ego that it is a form of falsehood and self-alienation.

How did we get here? We began with the Heideggerian notion that the psyche is essentially open to the world; did we really have to get to the conclusion that the world is necessarily an occasion for self-misunderstanding and alienation? In particular, I am concerned with the sense of inevitability, the sense that Freud's thought leads us, as though we were on train tracks, to this conclusion. Let me focus the problem by posing a specific challenge. In Lacan's account of the mirror stage, the child essentially misunderstands himself by attributing to himself the unity he sees in the mirror or the unity he intuits from his mother's gaze. He identifies with the unity of an image. But where does the unity in the image come from? There is nothing in the image itself that forces the child to see it as unified, and, no doubt, a psychotic child might see it as fragmented bits. Obviously, the child needs to have the capacity to see his image *as* unified, and he has the capacity to identify with that image. But why might this not be part of a healthy and legitimate process of psychological growth? Even if we grant that the unified image provides more of a sense of unity than the infant has formerly experienced—perhaps it does impose some order on what had hitherto been fragmented bodily experiences—why couldn't this be part of the healthy integration of the psyche? In short, the mother may attribute more unity to her child than the child has at that moment, but why not think of this as a step in a healthy parenting process by which the child acquires a true unity that is genuinely his? This is, of course, a best-case scenario. There are all sorts of occasions for misfire, for self-misunderstanding. But Lacan isn't talking about how things can go wrong some of the time; he is trying to give a constitutional account of the ego as such. His claim is that the ego is always and as such a *méconnaissance*. What legitimates that claim?

It is difficult to know how to engage Lacan with this question. Indeed, it is possible to view Lacan's oeuvre as a defense against the possibility of this question ever being raised. His style is enigmatic; his prose dense and slithering. There are no discrete arguments that one might examine step by step; rather, there are insights, declarations, aperçus, literary references, close readings of Freud, critiques, and sometimes caricatures of others, all woven together over the course of many pages. At its best, and it often is at its best, it is truly marvelous. But taken as a whole, it seems that either one somehow goes along with it or one gives up. As a result, the discussion of Lacan tends to divide into two categories. Either there are brilliant expositors of Lacan who may en route make striking applications of Lacanian thought,[2] or there are lame attempts to imitate. Lacan wrote in a style that was designed to be inimitable.[3] And he thereby attracted a generation of imitators. Phrases like "signifying chain," "metonymy," and "the unconscious is structured like a language" are moved about like pieces in a game. It is as though the imitators have to enact the movement of empty signifiers when that is what they are supposed to be talking about. However brilliant his insights, Lacan is the master who taught that psychoanalysts should have no disciples.

Truth be told, there is also bullying. French left-leaning intellectuals never seem to tire of holding Americans in contempt for their bourgeois naïveté. Lacan

---

2. For a sampling of outstanding work, see Dor (1999); Fink (1997); Gurewich (1999); Mathelin (1999); Nasio (1998a,b); Vanier (2000); Verhaeghe (2001); many works by Slavoj Žižek, most notably Žižek (1989); Zupancic (2000).

3. "I can pay myself the complement that through all the misadventures that my discourse encounters, here and certainly elsewhere, one can say that this discourse provides an obstacle to the experience of analysis being served up to you in a completely cretinous way" Lacan (1987, p. 174).

found it excellent sport to insist that the American school of ego psychology, which focused on the ego's ability to adapt to the world, was little more than an ideological rationalization of the American way of life. There is some truth to the charge, but the real question is whether the best accounts of ego development are also vulnerable to Lacan's critique.

How are we to get past all these defenses? It is in this context that Loewald is so liberating. For he starts with the same intuition that the psyche is fundamentally oriented to the world, and he agrees that one cannot understand the peculiar nature of this openness unless one works through the Freudian conception of a drive. But he moves in a fresh direction, and thereby exposes a Lacanian pretense: namely, the idea that the Freud-Heidegger train has to move along fixed tracks.

Psychoanalysis is founded on this irony: that which displays the animality of the human psyche mocks our attempts to represent ourselves as animals. We take our sexuality to reveal our animal nature, yet Freud's distinctive contribution is to show us how in our sexuality we are so unlike other animals. It is as though Freud plays the role of reluctant straight man: he keeps seeing that nature is playing a joke on us—indeed, that we *are* nature's joke—but he passes the joke along without fully getting it. After all, think of how he gets started. He wants to give an account of a class of people, hysterics, who in their essence both imitate and mock nature. They are blind, deaf, coughing, and lame, they lack sensations in certain parts of their bodies, are overly sensitive in others—and yet none of this fits accepted wisdom about anatomical reality. Is Freud really going to be able to give a biological account of this farce? In effect, he says to one of his early patients, Elizabeth von R., "Excuse me, Madam, I have to inform you that you are living out your sex life in your thigh. You have placed your genitals in your right thigh, just over *there.*"[4] How does he manage to say it with a straight face?

That's not all. He wants to give an abstract account of how this joke is possible. There is reason to do so, for if we don't understand this process, we will not understand how a talking cure is possible. We need to understand how the most elemental psychosomatic impulses can (or cannot) work their way up into language. Only then will we know how psychic change can occur through conversation. Nevertheless, there is reason to think that if Freud resorts to a biological model, he will also have to subvert it. For a purely biological account cannot possibly make sense of the bizarre phenomena he needs to explain. Freud does carry out the subversion, but he is not fully aware that this is what he is doing. One has to wonder whether he keeps himself unaware. If there is a single thread running through all of Freud's changing theories of the drives, it is the thought that although the current theory of the drives (whatever it may be) remains clouded by confusions and unknowns, no doubt some future research around the corner will clear it up.

---

4. Freud (1893–1895, pp. 144–158).

So, in "Instincts and Their Vicissitudes" (1915), a relatively early theorization, Freud waxes philosophical:

The true beginning of scientific activity consists . . . in describing phenomena and then in proceeding to group, classify and correlate them. *Even at the state of description it is not possible to avoid applying certain abstract ideas to the material in hand, ideas derived from somewhere or other but certainly not from the new observations alone.* Such ideas—which will later become the basic concepts of the science—are still more indispensable as the material is further worked over. They must at first necessarily possess some degree of indefiniteness; there can be no question of any clear delimitation of their content. So long as they remain in this condition, we come to an understanding about their meaning by making repeated references to the material of observation *from which they appear to have been derived, but upon which, in fact they have been imposed.* Thus, strictly speaking, they are in the nature of conventions—although everything depends on their not being arbitrarily chosen but determined by their having significant relations to empirical material, relations that we seem to sense before we can clearly recognize and demonstrate them. It is only after more thorough investigation of the field of observation that we are able to formulate its basic scientific concepts with increased precision, and progressively to modify them that they become serviceable and consistent over a wide area. Then, indeed, the time may have come to confine them in definitions. The advance of knowledge, however, does not tolerate any rigidity even in definitions. Physics furnishes an excellent illustration of the way in which even "basic concepts" that have been established in the form of definitions are constantly being altered in their content.[5]

But a quick glance through Freud's writings shows that he was never able to formulate the basic concept of a drive (*Trieb*) with "increased precision."

Five years later, as Freud introduces a major revision in his theory of the drives, in *Beyond the Pleasure Principle* (1920), he says:

> Here then is an opportunity for looking back over the slow development of our libido theory. . . . No knowledge would have been more valuable as a foundation for true psychological science than an approximate grasp of the common characteristics and possible distinctive features of the drives. But in no region of psychology were we groping more in the dark.[6] . . . In the obscurity that reigns at present in the theory of the drives, it would be unwise to reject any idea that promises to throw light on it.[7]

---

5. Freud (1915, p. 117). Loewald's emphasis; quoted in Loewald (1960, pp. 232–233).
6. Freud (1920, pp. 51–52). I substitute "drive" for the standard translation of "instinct" for *Trieb*. [The only exception is when I am citing the title of a translated essay, as in "Instincts and Their Vicissitudes" ("*Triebe und Triebschicksale*")].
7. Freud (1920, p. 53).

In *The Ego and the Id* (1923), he says, "The problem of
the quality of drive impulses and of its persistence
throughout their various vicissitudes is still very obscure
and has hardly been attacked up to the present."[8] In "An
Autobiographical Study" (1925), he continues in the
same vein: "There is no more urgent need in psychology
than for a securely founded theory of the drives on which
it might then be possible to build further. Nothing of
the sort exists, however, and psycho-analysis is driven to
making tentative efforts towards some such theory."[9]

Finally, in one of his last essays, "An Outline of Psychoanalysis" (1940), Freud says, "We have found that
drives can change their aim (by displacement) and also
that they can replace one another—the energy of one
drive passing over to another. *This latter process is still in-
sufficiently understood.*"[10] But it is precisely in this "latter
process"—change of aim, change of object—that Freud
originally invoked the concept of a drive to explain. Here
he is at the end of his career saying that it is that feature
of the drive he doesn't yet understand.

Freud wants to conceptualize the concept of a drive
(*Trieb*) along the lines of a biological instinct (*Instinkt*),
but it is precisely because the task can never be com-

---

8. Freud (1923, p. 44).
9. Freud (1925, pp. 56–57).
10. Freud (1940, p. 148; my emphasis). Gluttons for punishment
will also want to look to his late essay, "Analysis Terminable and
Interminable" (1937), where he says that the issues of how the drives
interact with each other "*are problems whose elucidation would be the
most rewarding achievement of psychological research*" (p. 243).

pleted that its solution seems just around the corner.[11]
Both drive and instinct are continuous sources of pressure, and Freud does want to capture the fact that human psychological life is *pressured*. The psyche is then
characterized teleologically as "an apparatus which has
the function of getting rid of the stimuli which reach it,
or reducing them to the lowest possible level."[12] The drive
does at least *imitate* the teleological structure of an instinct: it has an aim and is directed toward an object.[13]
But here the imitation becomes a mockery, for the drives
upend their own pretense to teleological structure. While
the sexual *instinct* in other animals will typically be directed toward a member of the same species of the opposite sex with an aim to achieve satisfaction in sexual
reproduction, the sexual *drive* in humans may or may
not be directed onto a member of the opposite sex, and
even if it is, it can move to fascination with the person's
clothes or an obsession with her shoes. In that obsession
the person may lose all interest in the biological sexual

---

11. As Jean Laplanche (1985, chapter 1) has pointed out, the *Standard Edition* translates both the German *Trieb* and *Instinkt* into the
English "instinct," thus flattening the important difference between
the two. See also Lacan's (1987) pioneering work.

12. Freud (1915), op. cit., p. 120. See Loewald (1960), op. cit.,
p. 233.

13. For Freud, the *object* of a drive is the thing through which and
in respect to which the drive seeks to attain its aim; the *aim* of a
drive is typically satisfaction, which for Freud tends to mean discharge. But, as we shall see, this changes with changes in Freud's
theory of the drives.

act; indeed, he might find it incomprehensible that he should ever be interested in such a thing. While the aim of a drive in the broadest sense remains satisfaction, the activity that achieves that aim can be transformed out of recognition. Who would have thought, for instance, that thinking about ideas might be a manifestation of a person's sexual life? Not only do the objects of the drive vary wildly, but, as we shall see, we cannot even remain secure about what the aim of a drive is.

What is marvelous about all this—literally: worthy of marveling at—is that Freud shows us that if we are going to help our patients engage in their own therapeutic action, we have to be willing to undergo a certain conceptual therapy ourselves. It is not enough that we understand our own unconscious wishes and inner conflicts; we have to free up the rigidities in our thought. This is nowhere more evident than in his magisterial *Three Essays on the Theory of Sexuality*, which is itself an invitation to undergo just this sort of therapy. For Freud, the ordinary conception of sexuality is itself the presenting symptom:

> Popular opinion has quite definite ideas about the nature and characteristics of this sexual drive. It is generally understood to be absent in childhood, to set in at the time of puberty in connection with the process of coming to maturity and to be revealed in the manifestations of an irresistible attraction exercised by one sex upon the other; while its aim is presumed to be sexual union, or at all events actions leading in that direction.

We have every reason to believe, however, that these views give a very false picture of the true situation.[14]

We tend to think we already know what human sexuality is; the only question is what counts as instances of it.[15] It is against this assumption that Freud's claim that infant's have a sexual life looks outrageous[16]; similarly, with his claim that hysterics are living out their sexual lives through their symptoms. But what Freud is discovering is not simply new items that fall under the concept of sexuality; he is discovering that the concept of sexuality must itself shift. Indeed, in our life with the concept we've become stuck, rigidly insisting that only *this* can be sexual!

In effect, what we've done is to pick out an un-problematic instance of sexuality—copulation—and say that and everything like that is sexual. The problem is that we've done nothing to get clear about what we mean by "like that." We tend to assume that in picking out a paradigm instance of sexuality, we are somehow isolat-

---

14. Freud (1905b, p. 135).
15. In philosophical terminology, the assumption is that we already know the intention, sense, or meaning of sexuality; the question is its extension or reference.
16. Anecdotally, I have found that those who are made angry by Freud's claim of infantile sexuality are often holding onto a fixed conception of sexuality and see him as attributing *that* to infants. Freud is then suspected of taking too much pleasure in debunking illusions about childhood. His project then looks objectionably reductionist. For his part, Freud is clear that we cannot attribute sexuality to children without altering what we mean by sexuality.

ing its essence, but this is an illusion. Indeed, it lies at the heart of human sexuality, properly understood, that we could never say in advance what its limits are.

For this reason it is a mistake to see Freud as emphasizing our animal nature. It is tempting to do so because we tend to assume we are rational animals, and sexuality, even as Freud construes it, certainly doesn't fall on the side of rationality! Thus it might seem that by emphasizing the centrality of sexuality in our lives, Freud is saying that we are little more than animals with pretensions.[17] But this is to misread Freud. It seems more accurate to see Freud as subverting the category of rational animal altogether. For if we had to place our sexuality anywhere, it would be on the "animal" side of this divide, but Freud shows us that it is precisely in our sexuality that we radically separate ourselves from the rest of the animal kingdom. It is only a slight exaggeration to say that there is nothing about human life we hold less in common with animals than our sexuality. We can imagine a bird happening to make a nest out of a lady's shoe; we cannot imagine her getting excited about it. The shoe-as-nest holds onto a biological function; the shoe-as-fetish leaves that behind.

What is it about human sexuality that makes the fetish a distinctly human possibility? From the point of view

---

17. Anecdotally, I have found that when people object to Freud, they often do so because they see him as a reductionist: insisting that because of the importance of our sexuality, we really are our animal natures. Because I think this is the wrong way to read Freud, I think this kind of objection is out of place.

of therapeutic action, there are three aspects of human sexuality that command our attention: first, the wide variability of the sexual object; second, the phenomenon of psychical overvaluation; and third, the fact that we make use of the variability and plasticity of the sexual object in the process of repression. As we shall see, living with these features catapults us into a position categorically different from all other animals.

The most important feature is the loose relation between the sexual drive and its object:

> We have been in the habit of regarding the connection between the sexual drive and the sexual object as more intimate than it in fact is. Experience of the cases that are considered abnormal has shown us that in them the sexual drive and the sexual object are merely soldered together— a fact which we have been in danger of overlooking in consequence of the uniformity of the normal picture, where the object appears to form part and parcel of the drive. We are thus warned to loosen the bond that exists in our thoughts between drive and object.[18]

The fact is, humans can direct their sexual attention to just about anything. Once they do that, there is a tendency to overvalue what they desire. Rather than being directed solely toward copulation, which is what one would expect if the sexual drive were just an animal instinct, the person becomes "intellectually infatuated . . .

---

18. Freud (1905b, pp. 147–148).

by the mental achievements and perfections of the sexual object and he submits to the latter's judgments with credulity. Thus the credulity of love becomes an important, if not the most fundamental, source of *authority*."[19] At this point in Freud's thinking, sexuality gives us reason to be skeptical of love—at least, skeptical of its first blush. Of course, it is nothing new to say that a person who is just falling in love will tend to idealize his love object. But, for Freud, the overvaluation does not have to be restricted to idealization; it can emerge in all sorts of intensifications of interest. So, for example, feeling intense nausea in the presence of a glass of water is also a form of overvaluation.[20] Even more interesting from a psychoanalytic point of view, the activity of psychical overvaluation can take the place of "normal" sexual activity, so that the overvaluing itself becomes the sexual activity.

The key to hysteria, Freud discovered, is that it makes use of these two aspects of sexuality in its own project of rejecting more obvious manifestations.[21] When the symptoms are bodily, it is as though these other parts of the body are "claiming that they themselves be regarded and treated as genitals."[22] But, more generally, the sexual life of hysterics is expressed in their symptoms.[23] Obviously,

---

19. Ibid., pp. 150–151.
20. See the case history Anna O. in Freud (1893–1895, pp. 34–35).
21. See, e.g., Freud (1905b, pp. 163–164).
22. Ibid., p. 153.
23. Ibid., pp. 163–164. See also Freud (1905a): "The symptoms of the disease are nothing else than the patient's sexual activity" (p. 115).

this is not how it is going to look to hysterics themselves; they will be suffering a cough, fatigue, an eating disorder, and so on.

But, then, the hysteric is the ideal candidate for irony. For there is a pretense, in this case it is a pretense to illness, that unconsciously mocks that which it pretends to be. Consider, for example, Dora's cough.[24] Dora puts it forward as a manifestation of physical illness; Freud diagnoses a condensation of meanings and sexual intensity. She identifies with Frau K.'s performing oral sex, perhaps she identifies with her father the smoker, perhaps she identifies with Dr. Freud inhaling one of his cigars, there are childhood patterns of sucking, and so on. What matters is the essential disparity between the pretense and the aspirations that are jointly getting expressed.

Freud tended to characterize this disparity in terms of hidden secrets:

> When I set myself the task of bringing to light what human beings keep hidden within them, not by the compelling power of hypnosis, but by observing what they say and what they show, I thought the task was a harder one than it really is. He that has eyes to see and ears to hear may convince himself that no mortal can keep a secret. If his lips are silent, he chatters with his fingertips; betrayal oozes out of him at every pore.[25]

---

24. Freud (1905a, p. 48).
25. Ibid., pp. 77–78.

But in terms of therapeutic action it is more helpful to conceive of the disparity in terms of aspiration and pretense. Because he took the hidden to be a secret, he casts himself in the role of detective. He uncovered Dora's secrets and laid them out before her, with famously disastrous results. But even if Dora had been a compliant and "grateful" patient and remained in treatment, this technique would have done nothing to bridge the gap between aspiration and pretense. What Dora needs is not the cognitive recognition of what her secrets are; she needs to bring the aspiring parts of her psyche into more direct communication with the pretending parts.

For this, interpretation needs to be indirect. If the analyst simply tells the analysand the meanings of her symptom, he is in danger of creating a new disciple. Even if the analyst's insights are accurate in terms of content, the analysand will emerge with a false sense of her problems, a false sense of who she is. The falsity in this case will lie not in the content of what she believes, but in how she lives with that content. In the name of psychic freedom she has ended up a follower of her analyst. The confusion will only be solidified if the analyst somehow teaches her that he wants no disciples: he is only there to promote her freedom.

To make the right kind of difference, an interpretation must focus on the disparity as it is being lived and help the analysand to work out for herself what it means. In Dora's case, we are not privy to the fine-grained details of how the case unfolded, but we can imagine a moment in which, while describing the outrageousness of her father's behavior, she breaks out coughing. Imagine an interpretation like, "You seem to be having a hard time swallowing all of that." Or, "It's enough to make you choke." Or, "You seem to be having a hard time coughing it all up." Exactly what one focuses on depends on the context, on a more fine-grained sense of what the symptom is. But all of these interpretations have in common that while they draw attention to the symptom as a meaningful act, they say nothing about what the meaning is. In this way it is left to the analysand to work out the meanings of her own meaningful act. It seems to me that Dora could have spent a good part of her analysis figuring out what it was about her life and situation that she was having a hard time swallowing.

Of course, in the transference the analysand might well think that the analyst is keeping a secret, that he knows what the cough means but he just won't tell. We will get to the transference in the next section. But for now it is worth noting, first, that while the analyst may have his hunches, associations, and tentative diagnoses, in an important sense he genuinely does not know. He does not have privileged access to the analysand's mind, and must therefore wait for the analysand to tell him what it means. Second, what the analyst is trying to "teach" is not the content of what the symptom means, but the activity by which one discovers for oneself what one's symptoms mean. That is why the interpretation needs to be indirect. It is not as though the analyst is being coy or secretive. There is literally nothing that could be communicated directly. For what the analyst is trying to communicate is not a hidden meaning that he knows but the analysand does not; he is trying to communicate the activity of bringing together the aspiring and pretending parts of one's psyche.

As an example, I have used a particular somatic symptom, but we can easily see that the overall structure applies widely. Character pathologies, to give a different example, are constructed around disparities between pretense and aspiration. But there is no reason to stop here. The disparity between pretense and aspiration goes to the heart of the human condition.

This is the essence of Freud's discovery about sexuality: *human sexuality makes us all candidates for irony.* For though hysteria is an extreme example, it presents a model that is pervasive in human sexuality; in repressing certain aspects of sexuality, we humans inevitably form a pretense. We use the variability of the sexual object and our capacity for overvaluation to form a pretense about our sexuality. Indeed, misleading ourselves about our own sexual life *is* our sexual life! That is, our sexual life gets expressed in the activities of repressing and distorting certain aspects of our sexuality. This is how humans fundamentally differ from the rest of the animal world: we inevitably stand in a relation to our own sexuality that make us candidates for irony. Other animals don't. Remember what Kierkegaard said about animals that walk on land with ancient fossils buried deep below; there is no irony there, because the animals do not pretend to be going on like their ancestors. (The comparison he drew was with contemporary Christians who do pretend to be going on like their forebears.) Other animals in their sexuality do not pretend to be going on like anything; we in our sexuality pretend to be going on like other animals. It is our pretension to animality that separates us from the rest of the animal world.[26]

In 1920 Freud fundamentally changed his theory of the drives. In particular, he substituted love for sexuality. To this day it remains unclear what this change means. The overwhelming consensus is that the change means very little. The widespread assumption is that it is Freud's introduction of the death drive that represents a radical departure. Love is then invoked as a more appropriate complement to so grand a master. On this point Lacan agrees with most American ego psychologists.

The notable exception is Loewald. He notes that in *Beyond the Pleasure Principle* Freud can't let go of a biological conception of the drive: "*It seems, then, that a drive is an urge inherent in organic life to restore an earlier state of*

---

26. An acquaintance once remarked to me that the reason the British were so promiscuous, as compared to Americans, is that they considered sexuality to be a strictly biological function. In this way, a certain pretense about sexuality facilitates a certain kind of manifestation of it. But the pretense also covers over the fact that this expression of sexuality also disguises from the participants the true nature of their sexuality. "They're fucking like animals!": ironically, that is something humans cannot do.

things which the living entity has been obliged to abandon under the pressure of external disturbing forces."[27]
This conception fits his old conception of the psychic
apparatus at aiming to reduce stimulation; and the death
drive only extends this idea by suggesting that the ultimate reduction is towards zero. The real problem lies in
understanding how to conceptualize the opposing
drive—and this is a task Freud evaded.

> It remained an insoluble problem for Freud to fit his
> life drive (or Eros) into his new definition of drive. . . .
> The inertia or constancy or unpleasure or Nirvana prin-
> ciple . . . fits perfectly with the death drive, insofar as
> the latter is "the expression of the inertia inherent in
> organic life." In this sense, the death drive is really noth-
> ing new, not a conception that should have taken psy-
> choanalysts by surprise. . . . What is new, and this does
> not seem to fit with the inertia principle . . . is the con-
> cept of Eros, the life or love drive.[28]

---

27. Freud (1920, p. 36; Freud's emphasis). See Loewald (1960,
p. 234).
28. Loewald (1971a), in Loewald (2000), op. cit., p. 62. See also,
Loewald (1973):

> The proposition of a duality of Eros and Thanatos, the life drive
> and the death drive, as a metapsychological assumption, for the
> first time establishes, although only tentatively, an independent
> psychic force that does not follow the constancy or Nirvana prin-
> ciple. The metapsychological (economic) meaning of pleasure, in
> the old pleasure principle, was the abolition or diminution of
> unpleasure or "stimulus tension," in pursuit of the return to a state

From Freud's point of view, the problem is this: he wants to hold onto a dualist conception of the drives. He has begun to formulate what he takes to be a radically new conception of one of the drives. But, then, how to conceptualize the complementary drive? Freud has always wanted to understand human conflicts in terms of conflicting drive-like forces. But now that he has captured what he thinks is so fundamental a force, he needs to find an equally fundamental conflicting force. But from Loewald's point of view, the problem is significantly different: the death drive is not as new as Freud thinks, but introducing love as a drive would require a radical reconceptualization. Freud himself does not see this.

Indeed, there is some question whether Freud hides this problem from himself by quickly resorting to philosophy. In the same year that he publishes *Beyond the Pleasure Principle*, 1920, he also publishes the fourth edition of *Three Essays on the Theory of Sexuality* (originally published in 1905). In the new preface to that edition, he says, "As for stretching the concept of sexuality which has been necessitated by the analysis of children and what are called perverts, anyone who looks down with con-

---

of absolute rest or "death." This tendency in psychic processes is now called the death drive. In this sense the death drive is nothing new, but merely a new conceptualization of the constancy principle. What *is* new in Freud's last instinct theory is the life instinct as a force or tendency *sui generis*, not reducible to the old pleasure–unpleasure principle." [p. 79; for uniformity of usage I have substituted the term "drive" for "instinct" in the Loewald quote to signal that he is talking about a *Trieb*, not an *Instinkt*.]

tempt upon psycho-analysis from a superior vantage-point should remember how closely the enlarged sexuality of psycho-analysis coincides with the Eros of the divine Plato."[29]

But this is the retrospective invention of a tradition. At the time he wrote the *Three Essays*, Eros was not on his mind. Indeed, the only glimpse one gets of a Platonic myth in the original edition is to distinguish traditional love from Freud's emerging conception of sexuality: "The popular view of the sexual drive is beautifully reflected in the poetic fable which tells how the original human beings were cut up into two halves—man and woman— and how these are always striving to unite again in love. It comes as a great surprise therefore to learn that there are men whose sexual object is a man and not a woman, and woman whose sexual object is a woman and not a man."[30] This fable is originally told by Aristophanes in Plato's *Symposium*. Although the story is coming out of Aristophanes' mouth, there is reason to believe that this is what Freud thought that Plato meant by Eros.[31] It is

29. Freud (1905b, p. 134).
30. Ibid., p. 136.
31. So, in *Civilization and Its Discontents* (1929), Freud says, "When a love-relationship is at its height there is no room left for any interest in the environment; a pair of lovers are sufficient to themselves, and do not even need the child they have in common to make them happy. In no other case does Eros so clearly betray the core of his being, his purpose of making one out of more than one; but when he has achieved this in the proverbial way through the love of two human beings, he refuses to go further" (p. 108).

thus amusing to see what distortions this fable suffered before it emerged as the popular view. First, Aristophanes' myth is meant to legitimize homosexual love. The earlier creatures from which humans emerged tended to have two sets of the same genitals, so when they were split apart their other half tended to be a human of the same sex. It is only because there were also some hermaphrodites that heterosexual love emerged among the new humans. Aristophanes was a comedian, and one would thus expect him to be at home with human foibles; but even he would be astonished to see his myth inverted so as to legitimate heterosexual love and make homosexual love problematic. Second, the popular view has erased the violence in the original story. Human life emerged because the earlier creatures were split in half by Zeus in punishment for their ambitious rivalry with the gods. Our belly buttons are the wounds from where we were sewn up after being split apart, and we are supposed to contemplate them the next time we get ambitious ideas. They are a reminder that if we don't watch out, we'll be hoping around on one foot and looking like the bas relief one sees on a gravestone.[32]

In short, before 1920 Freud treated what he took to be Platonic Eros as the opposite of what he was introducing as human sexuality. It is only after the introduction of the death drive in 1920 that he retrospectively decides that, in talking about human sexuality, he has all along been talking about Eros. It is a beautiful example at the

32. Plato, *Symposium* 189d–193b.

level of theory of the kind of revisionist history and covering over that Freud showed us was so typical of the human mind. Here are two more examples. From 1921:

> We are of the opinion, then, that language has carried out an entirely justifiable piece of unification in creating the word "love" with its numerous uses, and that we cannot do better than take it as the basis of our scientific discussions and expositions as well. By coming to this decision, psychoanalysis has let loose a storm of indignation, as though it had been guilty of an act of outrageous innovation. Yet it has done nothing original in taking love in this "wider" sense. In its origin, function and relation to sexual love, the "Eros" of the philosopher Plato coincides exactly with the love-force, the libido, of psychoanalysis.[33]

From 1924. "What psycho-analysis calls sexuality was by no means identical with the impulsion towards a union of the two sexes or towards producing a pleasurable sensation in the genitals; it had far more resemblance to the all-inclusive and all-embracing love of Plato's *Symposium*."[34] One could go on, but the important point is that there are no pre-1920 passages that even remotely make this point. As it turns out, this is of real theoretical significance. For the point is not merely the amusing one

33. Freud (1921, p. 91).
34. Freud (1924, p. 218).

that Freud is reinventing his past; rather, Freud is disguising from himself the pressing need for an articulated theory of love as a drive. Freud thinks he already has that theory, for he has lulled himself into thinking that love is just an extension of sexuality. In this way, he keeps at bay the realization that the introduction of love as a basic drive requires a significant reconceptualization.

One should expect, then, that Freud's thoughts on love will be an unfinished strand of his own conceptual development. But I suspect Freud was unconsciously motivated to leave that strand where it lay. For he took himself to be a natural scientist, but within what conception of nature could he be working if he took love to be one of its basic principles? And with what conception of science? *Christian science?* After all, what other "science" invokes love as a principle? Here is a symptom of conflict: on the one hand, Freud is breaking new ground in understanding human beings (aspiration); on the other hand, he wants to reassure himself and his readers that he is carrying on in the traditional methods of scientific investigation (pretense). But look at how wobbly the pretense is. When he introduces the death drive in *Beyond the Pleasure Principle*, there is speculation, consonant with biological research of his time, that there is an entropic tendency in living organisms to return to an inorganic state. It is as though he is just extending contemporary biological thought into the realm of psychology. But, then, what about its complement, love? How is he going to fit that principle into the positivist, reductionist, ato-

mistic aspirations of ninteenth century science? Freud is
virtually silent on the scientific status of love, and when
he does finally discuss it at the end of his career, it is by
switching to an ancient conception of science:

> The philosopher [Empedocles] taught that two prin-
> ciples governed events in the life of the universe and
> in the life of the mind and that those principles were
> everlastingly at war with each other. He called them
> φιλια (love) and νειϰos (strife). Of these two powers—
> which he conceived of as being at bottom "natural
> forces operating like drives, and by no means intelli-
> gences with a conscious purpose"—the one strives to
> agglomerate the primal particles of the four elements
> into a single unity, while the other, on the contrary
> seeks to undo all those fusions and to separate the pri-
> mal particles of the elements from one another.
> Empedocles thought of the process of the universe as
> a continuous, never-ceasing alternation of periods, in
> which the one or the other of the two fundamental
> forces again the upper hand, so that at one time love
> and at another strife puts its purpose completely into
> effect and dominates the universe, after which the
> other, vanquished, side asserts itself and in its turn de-
> feats its partner.
>   The two fundamental principles of Empedocles—
> φιλια and νειϰos—are, both in name and function, the
> same as our two primal drives, Eros and destructiveness,
> the first of which endeavors to combine what exists into
> ever greater unities, while the second endeavors to dis-

solve those combinations and to destroy the structures to which they have given rise.[35]

It is reassuring to go back to the wisdom of the ancients. Until, that is, one notices that one is drawing on *different* conceptions of nature and of science to hold onto the pretension that one is going on in the *same way* as a natural scientist.

It is easy enough to dismiss all this as (metaphysical) speculation. By and large, this is what the profession of psychoanalysis has done. Freud himself says that when it comes to his later theory of the drives he has "given free rein to the inclination, which I have kept down for so long, to speculation."[36] But is not this dismissal another kind of defense? Isn't there something about the nature of therapeutic action that Freud is trying to address when he invokes love as a drive? Shouldn't we be trying to work out what that is? This is the challenge Loewald takes up. It is his way of being a Freudian. (One might think that this was his way of *not* being a Freudian, given that Freud himself was so resistant to following out this line of thought. But maybe it was in this resistance that Freud ceased being a Freudian. In this alternative one can see how much freedom there is in creative repetition. There simply is no automatic answer to what is involved in being "true to Freud," and anyone who thinks there is has thereby ceased being a Freudian.)

---

35. Freud (1937, p. 246).
36. Freud (1925, pp. 56–57).

For Loewald, the move from sexuality to love is the movement from a closed to an open psyche. Because Freud saw that the object of the sexual drive was so variable, he hypothesized (unwisely) that originally the drive was independent of it. In this early conceptualization, the drives are inner stimuli with which the psychic apparatus tries to deal through discharge and diffusion. But as he reconceptualizes the drives, he sees them not only as fundamental to the mind, but as essentially directed to the world. Even the death drive, which might at first seem like a purely internal entropic force, is conceptualized as an urge to restore an earlier state of things that the organism has been forced to abandon "*under the pressure of external disturbing forces.*"[37] The death drive is thus manifested in reaction to environmental pressure, and one of the basic vicissitudes of the death drive is to turn itself outward as aggression.[38]

But the world-directedness of the psyche is even more evident in what Freud does say about Eros. By the time of his late work, "An Outline of Psycho-Analysis" (1940), he writes: "After long hesitancies and vacillations we have decided to assume the existence of only two basic drives, Eros and the destructive drive. . . . The aim of the first of these basic drives is to establish ever greater

---

37. Freud (1920, p. 36). Quoted in Loewald (1960, p. 234).
38. See Freud (1938): "So long as that drive operates internally, as a death instinct, it remains silent; it only comes to our notice when it is diverted outwards as a drive of destruction" (p. 150).

unities and to preserve them thus—in short, to bind together; the aim of the second is, on the contrary to undo connections and so to destroy things."[39] Unless one is steeped in Freud, it is difficult to see what a radical shift in his thinking this represents. For the drives can no longer simply be characterized as stimuli, and the psyche can no longer be characterized as simply in the business of reducing stimulation. Even more important, Freud abandons his long-held assumption that drives are essentially conservative: that they seek to restore an earlier state of things. As he puts it, "In the case of Eros (or the love drive) we cannot apply this formula."[40]

Interestingly, Freud had a way out and he didn't use it. There is one way he could have held onto the idea that the drives—even Eros—were essentially conservative. All he had to do, as he himself saw, was "presuppose that living substance was once a unity which had later been torn apart and was now striving towards reunion."[41] But this is precisely the account of Eros Freud himself invoked when he alluded to Plato's *Symposium*. In effect, Freud is discovering that Aristophanes was a conservative and ultimately he, Freud, is not. It is right here at the end of his career, twenty years after he first invoked Eros as a basic principle, that Freud sees that he needs to understand love as a *nonconservative* drive. Why? I suspect it's because he recognizes, however implicitly, that

---

39. Freud (1940, p. 148).
40. Ibid., p. 149.
41. Ibid.

to explain therapeutic action, one needs to make recourse to an inherently developmental force. There will be regressions and ups and downs, but one still needs to explain the tendency to respond to the psychoanalytic situation by growing in psychological complexity. There are acts of psychic unification and integration. However inchoately Freud understood this, he recognized that he needed to invoke some principle that would account for the phenomenon of psychological growth. He chose love, and thus, for him, love could not be a merely regressive force. It became, for him, the principle of growth, development, and therapeutic action.

In short, by the end of his career, Freud had completely changed the concept of a drive. It is not simply that he had different candidates for what counted as a drive, the very idea of what a drive is had undergone a massive shift. Loewald's point is that to take this shift seriously is to subvert some of our most basic assumptions. Notably, there is the assumption that now that we are interested in object relations, or in intersubjectivity, we can discard the theory of the drives as antiquated mechanics. Rather than seeing object relations as growing out of our theoretical past, it is often used as a means to repudiate it. This is the result of a false dichotomy. As Loewald says, "The issue of object relations in psychoanalytic theory has suffered from a formulation of the drive concept according to which drives, as inner stimuli are contrasted with outer stimuli."[42] So the choice can't

---

42. Loewald (1960, p. 236).

be between a drive theory of the inner workings of the individual mind versus an object relations theory of the person in a social environment. On Freud's mature theory, love and death are drives that structure object relations; similarly, if we are concerned with the world of internal objects. Internal object relations should not be thought of as a substitute for the drives, but a manifestation of them. Only thus will we be able to come to a deep understanding of their dynamism, the pressures they exert, and their vicissitudes.

In a similar vein, it is a psychoanalytic commonplace that while the ego is directed toward the external world, the drives are internal, making demands on the ego. Whatever validity this picture might have had in the early theory of the drives, it has to be abandoned. Indeed, as Loewald argues, it makes sense to think of the outer world as itself organized by the drives. "It would be justified to speak of primary and secondary processes not only in reference to the psychic apparatus but also in reference to the outer world insofar as its psychological structure is concerned."[43] That is, from a psychoanalytic point of view, we need to understand the outer world as it is experienced by a subject, and this experience will be organized by the drives. In an early paper, "Ego and Reality," Loewald takes issue with Freud's characterization of schizophrenic regression: "The schizophrenic does not primarily defend himself against reality by withdrawing from it, but reality regressively changes its character in

---

43. Ibid., p. 235.

such a way that the boundaries between ego and reality (and that also means the boundaries of ego and reality) become more fluid and to various degrees are lost."[44] Therapeutic action moves in the opposite direction. But how? Analysis may make use of controlled regressions, but for Loewald the therapeutic process essentially depends on the analysand's capacity to move across a psychological differential. As we have seen, the analyst is herself a manifestation of greater psychological complexity, and in this environment the analysand himself becomes more complex. It is this developmental push toward psychic organization that Freud invokes love to explain. For if the analyst is not suggesting a change or imposing one, then he is merely providing the occasion for one. The analyst's holding herself in this "neutral" position is itself an act of love, but we also need to understand what it is about the analysand that pushes him to reach out to this worldly complexity and develop in relation to it.

It is to Plato and Aristotle that we owe the idea that humans, unique among the animals, develop a *second nature*.[45] That is, humans are not born with fully developed characters or personalities; they develop them through early experiences in the social environment. But

---

44. Loewald (1951) in Loewald (2000), op. cit., p. 11.

45. The expression "*second nature*" I owe to John McDowell. See his fascinating discussion of these issues in McDowell (1994, pp. 78–84), and McDowell (1998, pp. 184–185, 188–189, 192–194, 197). For Plato's and Aristotle's discussions, see, most notably, Plato, *Republic* II–III; Aristotle, *Nicomachean Ethics* I–IV.

once character does develop, it is as though it is his own
nature. These character traits, Plato and Aristotle both
thought, are developed through imitation; it is through
imitation that we acquire habits and dispositions of the
psyche. It is striking that through the imitation we become more complex. Aristotle was interested in moral
psychology—on the acquisition of what he called the
excellences of human character, like courage.[46] He saw
that by imitating courageous acts we become courageous.
But this does not mean simply that we find it easier in
the future to stand fast before the enemy. Courage requires judgment as well as motivation. There may be circumstances in which the courageous thing to do is to
retreat or duck. A courageous person will have acquired
an almost perceptual capacity: she will see that in these
particular circumstances the honorable thing to do is
surrender.[47] Given that that is the courageous thing to
do, that is what she will want to do. For the true excellence of courage requires an integrated psyche. In other
circumstances, when surrender seems cowardly to her,
the idea of surrender becomes repugnant, psychologi-
cally impossible.

What is so striking about a human excellence, like
courage, is that there is no end to the level of psychological complexity it requires. Nineteenth century nov-

46. The Greek word "aretē" is standardly translated as "virtue," but
that word is so entangled with explicitly moral and religious connotations, that I prefer "excellence." It is because courage is part of
an outstanding human life that there is reason to live courageously.
47. See McDowell (1994, 1998).

els—those of Jane Austen, George Eliot, Tolstoy, and Dostoyevsky—are largely taken up with the endless difficulties in coming to see a situation correctly, coming to understand oneself honestly and figuring out a way to act that is true to self and world. The task is infinitely complicated by the awareness, pervasive through these novels, that we have to take account of unconscious motivations running through ourselves and others. Being courageous, then, is an endless task of becoming. As we keep interacting with the world (and with ourselves) in courageous ways, there is no end to the psychological complexity we may achieve. Courage is thus a subjective category: we become the subjects we are through the endless task of becoming courageous.

But here is a puzzle: why should *repeated* acts of my psychological capacity for courage result in a *development* of that capacity? Courage requires sensitivity—sensitivity to the endless nuances of this particular situation—and yet as I exercise my capacity of judgment over and over, my sensitivity improves. Not only do I deepen as a person, I enter ever more nuanced relations with the world. Why should this be? It is to answer this kind of question that Freud invokes love as a basic principle.

One reason Freud's theory of love has been ignored is that it seems ridiculous to take seriously the idea that love is really a basic principle of nature. Surely, we need to turn to natural scientists to find out what the basic principles of nature are. But what if we think about *second* nature? Now we are talking about the capacity to develop in character, personality, and psychological structure. What we need to explain is the capacity for growth in relationship to the environment—the capacity not only for internal organization, but for an ever more complex relationship with the environment. When one thinks about the development of the capacities for kindness or courage, or, say, the capacity to experience beauty or be creative, it no longer seems at all silly to say that what all these capacities have in common is a tendency toward forming ever more complex and differentiated unities. If you'd prefer to call that tendency by another name, that's up to you. There are, no doubt, all sorts of fruitful ways to theorize about psychological development. But from the perspective of developing a second nature, Freud's postulation of love as a drive should no longer seem utterly fanciful. Once one has formulated a theory like Freud's, then, from the perspective of the theory, *love can be seen as a necessary condition for the possibility of developing a second nature.* Now our second nature contains precisely the categories with which we develop ourselves as subjects. Thus it is an essentially subjective category. Love, then, becomes the condition for the possibility of subjectivity (that is, a condition for the possibility of ever forming ourselves into subjects).

Psychoanalysis is a peculiar extension of our capacity to acquire and develop a second nature. Psychoanalysis is not concerned with the development of any particular *moral* trait, but it is concerned with the *ethi-*

cal.[48] That is, it abjures "thou shalts" and "thou shalt nots," but it *is* concerned with the fundamental question, "How shall I live?" Ethics is the inquiry into how to live one's life. It is the fundamental question facing every human being (whether she likes it or not, whether she ignores it or not, and whether she evades it or not). Psychoanalysis is a peculiar raising of this fundamental question. It is tempting to think that psychoanalysis is not concerned with the development of any particular character trait like courage. This is because psychoanalysis, properly construed, does avoid all moralizing, and it is not concerned with the development of the superego in any particular direction. Still, it takes courage to face up to one's unconscious motivations, courage to face the motivations of others, courage to come to see the world in new ways. It takes courage to continue these processes without end. Perhaps we overlooked this insight because we have been living with a mere pretense of courage.[49] Perhaps we have avoided it because we have wanted to split off psychoanalysis as a "science" from anything that smacked of values. But if psychoanalysis is a science of our *second* natures, then it will have to have some kind of engagement with our values. Psychoanalysis is above all a special kind of commitment—a commitment to going on in a certain kind of a way. What is astonishing is that this kind of going on promotes the development of psy-

---

48. See Bernard Williams (1985). This distinction is also to be found throughout the ethical writings of Hegel.
49. This is in fact how Socratic irony begins. See Plato, *Laches.*

chological organization and complexity, and it promotes the development of freer, more complex and sensitive interactions with the world.

It is precisely this process of becoming analytically minded that Freud's theory of human sexuality on its own cannot explain. The sexual drive can explain the erotic transference onto the analyst, but it cannot explain how the analysand eventually acquires the capacity to analyze the transference for himself. That is, the sexual drive cannot itself explain the therapeutic action. One might draw on various conceptual resources to explain it, but this is essentially the task Freud assigns to love. Of course, we need to know the details of interactions that are involved. But love provides the overall framework in which analyst and analysand are mutually open to each other, and it grounds the idea that in the specific interactions, one can expect the analysand to grow in psychological organization and complexity.[50]

How are we to understand this growth? What does this peculiar form of courage—psychoanalytic activity—yield? We have already seen that human sexuality makes us all candidates for irony, and the neurotic is particularly unable to recognize the situation he is in. A good interpretation will, gently but firmly, bring this to light. One has to be careful here because there are defensive

---

50. Again, this is not the only way one can theorize about psychological growth or about therapeutic action. But these thoughts do show us, I think, what was underlying the theoretical choices Freud made in his conceptualization of love.

uses of irony. One can easily think of the ironic person
who uses his irony to keep himself and the world at bay.
Let us take another look at Dr. L.'s interpretation:[51]

> "Why would I want to tell you to fuck off? You haven't
> done anything but been there?
>   "Maybe that's why."
>   "Yes, you're the doctor, why haven't you cured me?
> I've been waiting for you to fix me."

There are two aspects of this moment that we are now in
a better position to see. First, *irony invites irony*. That is,
Dr. L.'s interpretation is ironic, drawing attention in an
open-ended way to a possible gap between Mr. A.'s pretense and the underlying psychic reality. But it is precisely the irony of the interpretation that invites Mr. A.
to become ironic with respect to himself. It is an occasion for the analysand to reinterpret retrospectively his
own just-uttered remark. "You haven't done anything but
been there" was originally uttered in a plaintive dead-
pan. The analyst's irony—"Maybe that's why"—puts the
analysand in a position where he can go back and ironize
his own utterance. The analysand is at last in a position
where he can begin an open-ended inquiry into what it
means *for him* that his analyst has done nothing for him
but been there.

Second, the act of becoming ironic is an act of uni-
fying the psyche. It is precisely because the original dead-

---

51. See Chapter 3.

pan use of "You haven't done anything but been there" was used as a defense, to ward off hostile and angry feelings, that the ironizing of that remark in the very moment in which it was deployed represents the undoing of the defense. The psyche then, as it were, rushes in to fill in the new meanings with a vibrancy that had hitherto been held at bay. In taking over the activity of nondefensive irony, Mr. A. not only comes to understand the appropriateness of the interpretation, but also fills it with living meaning. This is a reason to conceptualize love as a drive. We are trying to capture the quasi-instinctual force by which, in appropriate circumstances, the psyche grabs hold of meaning to organize itself.

In a truly ironic uptake the analysand not only grasps a meaning but also develops his own capacity for irony. The analysand begins treatment with little understanding of the gap between his aspirations and pretense. Even less does he understand how this gap is itself structuring his life. Through lovingly ironic interpretations, the analyst helps the analysand to bring this gap to light. But the point is not so much to learn the content of one's hidden aspirations or the pretentious nature of one's pretensions, it is to bring the aspiring and pretending parts of one's psyche into ever more vibrant communication. One does this finally by acquiring the capacity for analytic irony oneself. For structural change is not a once-and-for-all achievement. It is maintained through a perpetual undermining of rigidifying, and thereby alienating, pretenses. The fact that love is a basic drive suggests that if one does undermine the rigidities, one can count on the psyche to enter into ever more diverse communications with itself and with the world at large.

The transition from the sexual drive to love is precisely the transition from viewing humans as inevitable *candidates* for irony, to viewing them as capable of *becoming ironic* with respect to themselves. Freud was not explicitly aware that this is what he was doing when he introduced love as a basic drive. More than likely he recognized that the fact that humans develop in certain environmental circumstances needed explaining and he needed a complement to his newly discovered death drive. He reached back into the European speculative tradition and pulled out an enigmatic concept, Eros. Here "love" is functioning as little more than what Lacan called an enigmatic signifier. Thus Freud is re-creating, at the level of adult intellectual life, the kind of experience we have in childhood when parents bequeath to us remarks we cannot (yet) understand. We have the sense that we are being addressed and that something important is being said to us about who we are, but we can't quite make out what the meaning is. What is this thing called love? Whatever Freud explicitly had in his mind, the fact that we can make so much of his remarks—can deepen ourselves in relation to them—suggests that there is something true in his remarks. Freud once said that psychoanalysis was a cure through love.[52] This is something he could have meant by that.

---

52. Letter to Jung, December 6, 1906. See Freud and Jung (1974, pp. 12–13).

5

Transference as Worldiness

I am well adjusted.

You are going through an emotional crisis.

She is in the grip of transference.

Let I = Freud, You = Breuer, and She = Anna O., and this conjugation gives us an uncanny glimpse into the origins of psychoanalysis. By now it is well known that Breuer's treatment of Anna O. differed significantly from his report in the *Studies on Hysteria*. At the end of the case history, Breuer concludes:

I have already described the astonishing fact that from the beginning to end of the illness all the stimuli arising from the secondary [unconscious] state, together with their consequences, were permanently removed by being given verbal utterance in hypnosis, and I have only to add the assurance that this was not an invention of mine

181

which I imposed on the patient by suggestion. It took
me completely by surprise, and not until symptoms had
been got rid of in this way in a whole series of instances
did I develop a therapeutic technique out of it.[1]

In fact, Breuer got nowhere near the "end of her illness":
indeed, he got so entangled in it he fled. In 1932, ap-
proximately fifty years after the treatment, Freud wrote
a letter to Stephen Zweig in which he gave an account of
"what really happened to Breuer's patient."[2] "On the
evening of the day that all her symptoms had been
brought under control, he was called to her once more,
found her confused and writhing with abdominal cramps.
Asked what was the matter, she replied, 'Now comes
Dr. B.'s child.'" Breuer reacted to this dramatic event by
abandoning his patient and going on a vacation with his
wife. He never returned to psychoanalysis.

      Breuer and Freud have certainly been criticized for
the ways they treated young women, notably Anna O.
and Dora. But this also seems to be a case of scientific
fraud. For in the "Preliminary Communication" which
serves as the introduction to the *Studies*, Freud and Breuer
report, "We found, to our great surprise at first, that *each
individual hysterical symptom immediately and permanently disappeared when we had succeeded in bringing clearly to light the
memory of the event by which it was provoked and in arousing
its accompanying affect, and when the patient had described*

---

1. Freud (1893–1895, p. 46).
2. Here I rely on Peter Gay (1998, p. 67).

that event in the greatest possible detail and had put the affect into words."[3] But as they write this both authors know that their premier case ended in an emotional catastrophe, that not all her symptoms were cured. If they had bothered to think about it, they would have realized that if Breuer had stuck around to analyze the meaning of her hysterical pregnancy, it would have most likely falsified their theory. For the theory at that time was that hysterical symptoms were in every case expressing memories of actual events that had been so traumatic at the time that they were repressed. As they memorably put it, *"Hysterics suffer mainly from reminiscences."*[4] But what memory could possibly result in Anna O's pregnancy? What about the fact that she not only got "pregnant," she actually "gave birth to a baby"? As far as we know, Breuer and Freud kept themselves away from these obvious questions.

I do not mean to excuse this fraud by saying that the Freud I know is an honest man. Rather, I am trying to fit the sense of the man I have after reading and re-reading the entire corpus for over thirty years with this significant event. I do not believe that Freud set out deliberately to mislead his readers. So then what was he thinking? I suspect that at the time he was preoccupied by frustration with Breuer. He already suspected that the repressed memories were sexual, and he no doubt saw Anna O.'s symptom as providing confirmation of the theory he could not yet utter. It must have been frustrat-

---

3. Freud (1893–1895, p. 6; Freud's emphasis).
4. Ibid., p. 7; Freud's emphasis.

ing to him that Breuer fled just when the case was open-
ing up its sexual meaning, and it must have been even
more frustrating to have to hold his tongue, while this
important symptom was relegated to the privacy of
Breuer's life. "Better this, than nothing," I suspect he
thought. Within two years, Freud had given up the theory
of repressed memories, given up the cathartic method,
and had gone on to other therapeutic techniques.

Still, it is in this hothouse of shock, embarrassment,
and covering-over that Freud gives birth to the concept
of transference. One has to wonder whether the personal
turmoil suffered by the analysts has not (unconsciously)
affected the way they conceptualize what they experience.
By now we are ready for the idea that transference involves a certain pretense, but we first need to investigate
whether the concept itself is somehow keeping us in the
dark about the phenomenon. But how might we think
about distortions that occur in the very concepts with
which we think? Clearly, conceptual therapy is in order.

Here is how Freud first introduces the concept:

> Transference on to the physician takes place through a
> *false connection.* I must give an example of this. In one of
> my patients the origin of a particular hysterical symp-
> tom lay in a wish, which she had had many years earlier
> and had at once relegated to the unconscious, that the
> man she was talking to at the time might boldly take the
> initiative and give her a kiss. On one occasion at the end
> of a session, a similar wish came up in her about me.
> She was horrified at it, spent a sleepless night, and at

the next session, though she did not refuse to be treated, was quite useless for work. After I had discovered the obstacle and removed it, the work proceeded further; and lo and behold! the wish that had so much frightened the patient made its appearance as the next of her pathogenic recollections and the one which was demanded by the immediate logical context. What had happened therefore was this. The content of the wish had appeared first of all in the patient's consciousness without any memories of the surrounding circumstances which would have assigned it to a past time. The wish which was present was then, owing to the compulsion to associate which was dominant in her consciousness, linked to my person, with which the patient was legitimately concerned; and the result of this *mésalliance*—which I describe as a "false connection"—the same affect was provoked which had forced the patient long before to repudiate this forbidden wish. Since I have discovered this, I have been able, whenever I have been similarly involved personally, to presume that a transference and a false connection have once more taken place. Strangely enough, the patient is deceived afresh every time this is repeated.[5]

It takes nothing away from the strangeness of the phenomenon to note that it is being conceptualized in such a way that it is all the patient's doing. The *very idea* of transference (as it is conceptualized here) is that the

---

5. Ibid., pp. 302–303; Freud's emphasis.

patient takes emotions that were appropriately directed toward another person and inappropriately *transfers* them onto the doctor. The doctor has nothing to do with it. So although Anna O.'s "pregnancy" is not acknowledged in the book, by the end Dr. Breuer has been absolved of "paternity." Note, too, that in the example that Freud gives to illustrate the concept, the treatment seems to be going badly. Freud presents the case in the light of what he understood after he had figured it out. But in terms of the order of discovery, what Freud first encounters is an uncooperative patient. As he reports it, while she didn't absolutely refuse to be treated, she was "quite useless for work." So, in the first instance, Freud is trying out a relatively new and untested therapy, and it apparently isn't working. It is not surprising that as he tries to figure it out, he will formulate a concept that emphasizes how the patient is behaving irrationally toward him. Finally, if the concept did not have this tinge, the whole model of the patient–doctor relationship might be called into question. For if the patient isn't just exhibiting the disease she already has independently of the doctor, and if the doctor isn't just treating an antecedently existing disease, then what *are* they doing together? Given Anna O.'s pregnancy, this should have been an urgent question.

Freud's greatest contribution to the conceptualization of transference is in the postscript to the Dora case, and it is there to explain a botched job. Freud acknowledges that his treatment of Dora was a failure and he invokes the concept of transference to explain it.

There must, then, be a question of whether some plea for justification isn't creeping into the formulation of the concept. At the same time he is treating Dora, he is writing *The Interpretation of Dreams*. In that work, Freud analyzes a now-famous dream, the dream of Irma's injection, which discloses two powerful unconscious wishes of his own: a wish simply to get rid of recalcitrant women patients and a wish to vindicate himself. By Freud's own reckoning, these wishes should have been alive at the time he was treating Dora. (Indeed, if he had been aware of the phenomenon of countertransference, he might have used his dream as a means of holding on through the storms of treating Dora.) Freud tells us that he first thought of writing up the Dora case under the title "Dreams and Hysteria," for it supported his theory of dreams.[6] The postscript is written a few years later, yet however magnificent his insights into transference are, it is also true that Freud is trying to vindicate himself for a patient he actually did get rid of.

In the same postscript in which he conceptualizes transference, he also reports that fifteen months after Dora abruptly ended her treatment, she came back to Freud and asked him to resume treatment. "One glance at her face, however, was enough to tell me that she was not in earnest over her request."[7] One glance? If Freud has taught us anything, it is to be suspicious of anything

---

6. Freud (1905a, p. 10).
7. Ibid., p. 120.

we think we can see with just one glance. He is elsewhere the master of showing us that anything she might actually be showing in her face will have layers of meanings. He concludes with a sentence that should be taped to every analyst's desk to serve as a perpetual warning: "I do not know what kind of help she wanted from me, but I promised to forgive her for having deprived me of the satisfaction of affording her a far more radical cure for her troubles."[8] In the contest for most-awful-sentence-ever-written-by-Freud, this is the hands-down winner. However he failed Dora, the concept of transference is being written by an angry man seeking justification.

There is also a question whether Freud needed to flee Dora just as Breuer fled Anna O. For it seems that Dora, too, had gotten herself "pregnant." Nine months after Herr K.'s seductive proposal by the lake, Dora came down with stomach cramps, which, at the time, were diagnosed as appendicitis. Freud suspected this too was a hysterical pregnancy. But, then, if he is thinking of transference as that which is coming around the bend, might he not have been dimly aware that if he hung on for nine months he was likely to suffer the same catastrophe that Anna O. inflicted on Breuer? We certainly know from the dream of Irma's injection that Freud is dreaming about injecting a dirty syringe into his woman patient. Is it any wonder that he in effect said, "Let me out of here! I'm not the father! It's only transference!"?

---

8. Ibid., p. 122.

There is certainly room to wonder whether Freud re-enacted Breuer's flight.

Freud dubs "transference" the moment in the analysis he didn't see coming.[9] One might think therefore that transference will be conceptualized as momentary, abrupt, intrusive, pathological, solely the patient's production, and, above all, disruptive of the therapeutic action. But Freud is too creative a thinker for that to be the

---

9. See Freud (1905a, pp. 118–119):

> I did not succeed in mastering the transference in good time. Owing to the readiness with which Dora put one part of the pathogenic material at my disposal during the treatment, I neglected the precaution of looking out for the first signs of transference, which was being prepared in connection with another part of the same material—a part of which I was in ignorance. . . . But when the first dream came, in which she gave herself the warning that she had better leave my treatment, just as formerly she had left Herr K.'s house, I ought to have listened to her warning myself. . . . But I was deaf to this first note of warning, thinking I had ample time before me, since no further stages of transference developed and the material for the analysis had not yet run dry. In this way the transference took me unawares, and, because of the unknown quantity in me which reminded Dora of Herr K., she took her revenge on me as she wanted to take her revenge on him, and deserted me as she believed herself to have been deceived and deserted by him. Thus she acted out an essential part of her recollections and phantasies instead of reproducing them in the treatment.

Jacques Lacan has argued to interesting effect that transference is resistance in the analyst. See Lacan (1985, 1993). I don't ultimately agree with his conclusion, but it does present a serious challenge to the conceptualization of transference.

whole story. And what we are concerned with ultimately is not Freud, but the legacies that are unconsciously on our minds. It is easy enough to use a study of the past defensively: "Those were the old days, these are the new, we certainly don't think *that* anymore!" It is much more difficult to probe our past to find something present, hidden in ourselves.

Freud also invokes the transference to explain a peculiar phenomenon of psychoanalysis: patients get better *after the treatment is over*! "It is true that the symptoms do not disappear while the work is proceeding; but they disappear a little while later, when the relations between patient and physician have been dissolved. The postponement of recovery or improvement is really only caused by the physician's own person."[10] We can imagine a medical doctor telling a patient, "Take two aspirin and you'll feel better by morning"; the doctor goes home, and the patient feels better in the morning. But what are we to make of the idea that it is essential to the cure that the doctor go home? Doesn't this make a mockery of the idea of medical treatment? It's as though the doctor's being there is part of the disease. If the doctor showed up with smallpox, it might be essential for him to go home. But is this how we are to understand the gift that the psychoanalyst brings to his patient?

> I must go back a little in order to make the matter intelligible. It may be safely said that during psychoanalytic

---

10. Freud (1905a, p. 115).

treatment the formation of new symptoms is invariably stopped. But the productive powers of the neurosis are by no means extinguished; they are occupied in the creation of a special class of mental structures, for the most part unconscious, to which the name of *transferences* may be given.[11]

Whence the confidence that there are no new symptoms? Officially, the idea is that the patient's creative powers will become so absorbed in the analysis that she won't have energy to form symptoms outside. Her family is spared an outbreak of yet some new disease. But why not say that, indeed, the patient will develop new symptoms, only this time the symptoms will entangle the doctor? But if the patient is getting sick all over again, this time with her doctor, how are we to understand this as part of any therapeutic action? "Transference" is the name Freud lays down to keep this idea at bay. He calls it a "special class of mental structures"—that which shall not go by the name "new symptom."

But what makes this class of mental structures special? We can see Freud struggling to defeat the idea that, in the case of psychoanalysis, the doctor makes the patient worse rather than better. Even if we are not so concerned with that problem ourselves, we ought to be suspicious of the aura of specialness with which transference is introduced. For there is a lingering question of what transference we have to the concept of transference.

---

11. Ibid., p. 116.

For if transference is that special thing with which we analysts have to deal—if, indeed, our identity as analysts is constructed around our special ability to handle this special thing—there is a danger that by naming it, and by naming it as our special thing we will be seduced into thinking we understand it better than we do.

Freud gives this famous account:

> What are transferences? They are *new editions or facsimiles* of the tendencies and phantasies which are aroused and made conscious during the progress of the analysis; but they have this peculiarity, which is characteristic for their species, that they replace some earlier person by the person of the physician. To put it another way: *a whole series of psychological experiences are revived,* not as belonging to the past, but as applying to the person of the physician in the present moment. Some of these transferences have a content which differs from that of their model in no respect whatever except for the substitution. These, then—to keep to the same metaphor—are merely new *impressions or reprints.* Others are more ingeniously constructed: their content has been subjected to a moderating influence—to *sublimation,* as I call it—and they may even become conscious, by cleverly taking advantage of some real peculiarity in the physician's person or circumstances and attaching themselves to that. These then will no longer be new impression, but *revised editions.*[12]

---

12. Ibid., p. 116.

So transference, on this account, is both new and not new. It is new in the sense that it is a special structure, not the creation of a new symptom; it is not new in the sense that it is only a new edition, a facsimile, a new impression or reprint of something old. In this way, Freud doubly denies that the doctor is introducing the disease: "The patient had it anyway, and in any case what's happening isn't a symptom, it's *transference!*"

But new editions of what? If we don't know what the editions are editions of, we don't know what transference is. Freud says that they are new editions of a whole series of psychological experiences. How are we to make sense of this idea of a whole series? Freud needs to give content to the clinical fact that transference tends not to be an isolated atomic experience, but rather occurs in a holistic emotional environment. So, for example, if Dora's abrupt termination of the treatment is a transferential repetition of the slap she gave Herr K., it doesn't come on completely on its own, like a nervous tick. Rather, the metaphorical slap comes embedded in an emotional aura in which Freud is beginning to take on a Herr K.–like quality. How are we to understand this aura?

One might say that, for Dora, Freud is coming to take up Herr K.'s position. Dora does not actually think that Freud is Herr K., but he is coming to take on qualities that put him in a structurally analogous position for her. That is what Freud says he didn't see coming. But then how are we to understand the idea of a position? The idea of position is unintelligible without a corresponding idea of a space in which that position is located.

If there is a Herr K. position, in what space is this position located and in relation to what? We are thus led naturally to the idea that in Dora's world Freud is coming to take up a Herr K. position. Now we certainly do not yet understand what we mean by "a world," but there is something that is coming clearer about transference. Namely, that to give an account of transference it is not enough that we account for the various inhabitants of Dora's world; we need to account for the fact that she has a world at all.

For Dora's transference is manifest in the *worldiness* of her world.[13] That is, the situation cannot be merely that Dora has unconsciously assigned Freud to a Herr K. position. Even if she has, there is a further question about what must her experience be like, such that it could have a Herr K. position in it. What is the structure of meanings such that it makes sense to talk of a Herr K. position? Or, rather, what is involved in there being such a structure? It is important to get a glimpse at least of what a tricky question this is to answer. At first one might think that Dora associates Herr K. with a certain feature, say smoking a cigar. When she sees Freud smoking a cigar, she "transfers" her Herr K.–like feelings onto him. But this isn't going to answer the question of how there could be a Herr.K.–like position in the first place. Nor will the problem be solved if we add on more properties. The issue cannot be captured in terms of the projection of properties. Rather, on the basis of certain experiences,

---

13. For students of Heidegger, what we are concerned with here is a (largely unconscious) *ontic* manifestation of worldiness.

Dora comes to *orient* Freud in Herr K.–like ways. But orientation isn't a property, it is a world-structuring, and we do not yet understand what this could be.

In short, there is still much about transference that we don't understand. It is certainly true that we are more aware of the countertransference than Freud was, and we have learned to deploy it as a clinical tool. We are aware of the transference–countertransference field, the interplay of transference and countertransference, transference as a total situation.[14] These represent important clinical and theoretical advances, but if we assume we have thereby answered the question about the worldiness of transference, we keep ourselves in the dark. If transference raises questions of worldiness, we are not going to answer them by saying we are concerned with the total situation: the question re-arises, What could we mean by a *total* situation? What is it about the totality that makes it total? What is it about a situation that makes it a situation? Nor is the question answered by saying, "We're not only concerned with transference, we're also concerned with the countertransference." Whatever problems about worldiness that occur in transference are going to reoccur around the countertransference. It is of no help to say we are talking about the transference—countertransference field. The question only re-arises about the field: What is it about the field that makes it a field?

This problem was hidden from Freud and it is still largely ignored. Freud was so concerned with capturing

---

14. See, e.g., Betty Joseph (1989).

transference as a phenomenon *in* the world, that he failed to notice the worldly nature of transference itself. Indeed, on its surface, the idea of transference seems to presuppose a determinate world across which a transfer occurs. So, an emotion originally directed toward one person is transferred (across space and time) onto Freud. This is what he called the "false connection." This is why transference seems to be a phenomenon in the world. If Freud hadn't presupposed a given world, there would be no basis for conceptualizing what was happening as a transfer of a certain emotion from one person to him. In this way, the surface idea covers over a deeper meaning in which transference is not a phenomenon in the world, but is itself a form of world-structuring. In general, we have been so concerned with how Freud got this aspect of transference right, this aspect wrong, and so on, that we don't notice we are working in the same context. We are treating transference as a phenomenon and then trying to figure out what its properties are. But phenomena show up in the world, the world itself is not another phenomenon. Nor is worldiness. So if transference is worldiness itself, then "it" is not a phenomenon in the world. Rather, it is more like the structuring condition in which phenomena show up for us. This cannot be uncovered along the lines of discovering the properties of an object. To understand transference, we need to understand some peculiar features of the worldiness of the world.

The problem is made even more difficult by the fact that psychoanalysts, psychotherapists, and psychologists tend to live with confused ideas of subjectivity and objectivity. Thus when one uses a phrase like "Dora's world," there is a tendency to think (1) what is meant is Dora's *subjective* world; and (2) that because it is a subjective world, it must therefore be *intra*psychic. It must be in her mind. But then how could Freud be part of Dora's world? It would seem that Dora would have to project her internal image of Herr K. out onto Freud and then introject this new figure. But these assumptions of projection and introjection are being dictated by an understanding of "subjective world" that is itself unexamined. Before we can understand transference, we need to reexamine what we could mean by "subjective world." To do this, we need to put aside the (Cartesian) assumption that by "subjective" we must mean inner, and by "objective," outer.

This is not the place to rehash Heidegger.[15] But I do want to take up his idea that what we most essentially are is "being-in-the-world." We are creatures who are essentially engaged in the world, and we reveal who and what we are in the nature of our engagements. In our everyday life, the worldiness of the world is not explicitly apparent to us. I get up sleepily and make my way to my daily morning appointment with Dr. Freud. I knock on the door, go in, and today I have nothing much to say to him. When will the hour be over? In doing this, I don't

---

15. In any case, rehashes tend to be a bore. For any reader interested in these issues, I strongly recommend "The Worldiness of the World," part one, division I, chapter 3 of Heidegger (1927).

have to think, "Dr. Freud is a doctor, and doctors are a class of people who help others when they are sick. I am sick and am seeking his health. There are other kinds of doctors. There is also a society in which Dr. Freud and I are located. It's December 1899. Thousands of miles to west is New York City. Maybe I'll go there some day." There are all sorts of thoughts I don't have to have, but inhabiting such a totality of relevant facts and things is the implicit background in the context of which I am able to carry out my almost-thoughtless act. "World itself is not an innerworldly being, and yet it determines innerworldly beings to such an extent that they can only be encountered and discovered and show themselves in their being because 'there is' world."[16] That is, objective things make themselves manifest only in a larger context of meanings and significances.

It is part of the objective world that Freud saw patients at Bergasse19, Vienna, at the turn of the twentieth century. It is also part of Dora's world that she went to see him there. Not in her mind or as an internal image, but *there*, at Bergasse19. Here the subjective world is not being characterized as an nonoverlapping alternative to the objective world, rather it is trying to capture the subjectivity of a subject or of a particular group of subjects. It tries to capture the idea of a totality of relevance and meaning for a given subject. What is the world like for her?

Dora is neurotic—she is not psychotic, delusional, catatonic, or autistic. Thus Bergasse19 is as much part of

---

16. Heidegger (1996, pp. 67–68).

her world as it is the objective world. Indeed, to a large extent, the objective world is her world. Thus the neurosis, not psychosis. She knows where she lives, she knows where Freud lives, and she knows how to get there. Of course, there may be all sorts of meanings that are peculiar to her of which she is aware. The cigar smoke emanating from the window may consciously remind her of her father. Freud showed us that there will be many peculiar associations of which she is unaware. But meanings alone do not make a world. What Freud also showed us—of which he was at most dimly aware—is that these meanings themselves tend to form a structured totality. The structure of this totality is itself largely unconscious.

To understand transference as worldiness, we have to understand two aspects of transference that Freud did bring to our attention: transference as day-residue and transference as transference-neurosis.

We learn from the dream process that dreams will often form around some seemingly indifferent event of the day. Freud happened to walk by a bookstore and saw a botanical monograph in the window; that night he dreamed of a botanical monograph. When he analyzed this seemingly indifferent dream, it went to the core of his being.[17] One might say that all of Freud's fundamental conflicts were locked in this one innocent image. How could this be? Freud invokes transference, and Loewald insists upon this conception of transference for under-

---

17. Freud (1900, pp. 165–188).

standing the therapeutic action. Here is a passage from
The Interpretation of Dreams:

> We learn from [the psychology of the neuroses] that an
> unconscious idea is as such quite incapable of entering
> the preconscious and that it can only exercise any effect
> there by establishing a connection with an idea which
> already belongs to the preconscious, by transferring its
> intensity onto it and getting itself "covered" by it. Here
> we have the phenomenon of "transference" which pro-
> vides an explanation of so many striking phenomena in
> the mental life of neurotics. The preconscious idea which
> thus acquires an undeserved degree of intensity, may
> either be left unaltered by the transference, or it may
> have a modification forced upon it, derived from the
> content of the idea which effects the transference.[18]

Now Freud is here talking about the dream process, so
he describes transference as an intrapsychic phenomenon. But there is nothing peculiarly intrapsychic about
the process. It might happen as Freud walks past the
bookstore, or as he passes it every day. The book itself
may take on a charged significance for him, the meaning of which he knows not what. Ironically, precisely because the book didn't have much meaning for him to
begin with, it comes to have overwhelming meaning for
him. The mind used the relative indifference of the book

---

18. Ibid., pp. 562–563. See also p. 564. Quoted by Loewald (1960,
p. 247).

to latch onto it and give it significance. Another person with concerns similar to Freud's might have latched onto virtually anything else.

So here we have transference as a phenomenon that unconsciously bequeaths idiosyncrasy to a shared public world. Everyone in Vienna can agree that there is a book in the store window, but in those peculiar meanings Freud is on his own. There is no reason why this idiosyncracy cannot be pervasive: all sorts of people and things become occasions for unconscious transferences of meaning. The day's experiences "offer the unconscious something indispensable—namely the necessary *point of attachment* for a transference."[19] In healthy circumstances this can lend a richness and texture to life, but in pathological circumstances life itself becomes distorted. Therapeutic action is the process of moving from the latter to the former.

In pathological circumstances, the world itself becomes distorted. This is because the world is itself manifest in the relations of significance of things in the world. Transference will inevitably disturb those relations. For transference is transference not only of meanings, but also of intensity and significance. Freud was able to make his experience creative: he managed to dream about the book, then analyze the dream, then, really, invent the interpretation of dreams as the extended analysis of that dream. Not everyone is so lucky or so psychically creative.

---

19. Ibid., p. 564. Quoted by Loewald (1960, p. 247).

Consider a patient I treated, Mr. B. One day he happened to have a difficult time going to the bathroom
in a public toilet. At least, so it seemed. He was in a
stall when a few others came into the men's room
loudly laughing and sharing stories. He felt his
muscles cramp. The next time he went to a men's
room, he found that he was worried that others
might burst in. He couldn't relax his muscles. Now
life became difficult for him because he didn't want
to go to the men's room any more. If he had to go
to the bathroom, he would hold it. But now he
started to get filled with anxiety that he wouldn't be
able to hold it. Would he be able to get home before he soiled himself? Soon he began structuring
the day around avoiding this possibility. He would
get up early and drink cup after cup of coffee. He
hoped that would empty him out for the day. Then
he would avoid lunch. Social life became structured
around avoiding such embarrassing occasions. He
became afraid to travel in planes and trains. He developed hypersensitivity in his ears: could *anyone* be
listening? And so on. It was not long before every
aspect of his life was organized around going to the
toilet, and, at least as far as he could tell, it began
with one loud outburst in the men's room.

Even without entering the analysis of Mr. B., one
can see how deeply disturbed the relations of significance
in his world have become. He can recognize the shared,
social meaning of an invitation to lunch, but for him it is

also experienced as a threat. He is so worried about it that he tries to position himself in out-of-the way places when it comes to be late morning. God forbid someone should invite him for a cup of coffee. Really, he had no idea what the source of his terror was, but life was now organized around avoiding terror; and his world was structured via his sense of gastrointestinal threat.

> Or consider a previously discussed patient, who inhabited a disappointing world—I shall call her Ms. C.[20] One can think of a person's world as the total structure of her possibilities—and all of Ms. C.'s possibilities were structured so that they would be experienced as disappointments. In the transference she was disappointed that I would only be her analyst. Why wouldn't I just lie down on the couch next to her? Why couldn't we go out to dinner together? She was regularly furious with me because she imagined seeing me talking to other women in the courtyard. She regularly "saw" my car parked somewhere or other and was sure I was with another woman. Why couldn't we do this? Why would I do that with anyone but her. She was hurt and dejected when I refused to accept an expensive Christmas gift, and so on.

Now what is striking about this transference is not merely the peculiar role I am assigned, but that I am

---

20. See Chapter 2.

assigned a role that sustains a world. It is not simply that I am another disappointing figure, but I secure the world as disappointing. It was only late in the analysis that she came to see it wasn't because I refused to do these nonanalytic acts that she was disappointed, but rather that she wished for these nonanalytic acts in part to maintain a sense of disappointment with me. But to gain this perception, she had to change her world. She had to come to see that the world itself was not structured by disappointment, but that she had been active in so structuring it.

This is a moment in which the world itself shifts: there is, as it were, a possibility for new possibilities. This "possibility for new possibilities" is not an ordinary possibility, like all the others, only new. The fact that Ms. C. inhabited a world meant that she lived amidst what for her were all the possibilities there were. For her, there simply was no possibility of experiencing, say, a promotion as a success rather than as a disappointment. One cannot simply add that possibility to Ms. C.'s world piecemeal, as though everything else about her can remain the same, only now it is possible for her to experience promotion as a success. Rather, the order of possibilities itself has to shift so that now success becomes an intelligible and welcome aspect of life. The possibility for new possibilities is not an addition of a special possibility to the world; it is an alteration in the world of possibilities.

Freud was not himself explicit about the world-structuring nature of transference, but it is implicit in his interpretation of his own dreams, where what he uncovers are not isolated wishes but structuring relations of love, hate, and demand for recognition. He called them phantasies. I don't think we understand fundamental phantasies unless we see them as world-structuring. It is also implicit in his insistence upon the importance of myths, notably the Oedipus myth, for understanding the human psyche. For myths are themselves concretions that try to represent structuring totalities. But the place where the worldiness of transference becomes clearest is in the transference neurosis.

Here is what Loewald says about the transference neurosis:

[The] indestructibility of unconscious mental acts is compared by Freud to the ghosts in the underworld in *The Odyssey*—"ghosts which awoke to new life as soon as they tasted blood", the blood of conscious-preconscious life, the life of contemporary present-day objects. . . . The transference neurosis, in the technical sense of the establishment and resolution in the analytic process, is due to the blood of recognition, which the patient's unconscious is given to taste so that the old ghosts may reawaken to life. Those who know ghosts tell us that they long to be released from their ghost life and led to rest as ancestors. As ancestors they live forth in the present generation with their shadow life. Transference is pathological insofar as the unconscious is a crowd of ghosts, and this is the beginning of the transference neurosis in analysis: ghosts of the unconscious, imprisoned by defenses but haunting the patient in the dark of his de-

fenses and symptoms, are allowed to taste blood, and
are let loose. In the daylight of analysis the ghosts of the
unconscious are laid and led to rest as ancestors whose
power is taken over and transformed into a newer intensity of present life.[21]

Note that Freud and Loewald depict the unconscious in
worldly terms. The ghosts in *The Odyssey* live in an underworld; they interact with each other and their relations
are structured by the world they inhabit. To paraphrase
the novelist L. P. Hartley, in *The Go-Between*, the unconscious is like a different world; they do things differently
there.[22] Now even when an individual ghost comes to
haunt our world, he comes with a message from the other
world. There are at least intimations of a completely different order of structuring of relations. We glimpse an
other-worldly sense of worldiness.

This is an aspect of transference that is often overlooked: the figures are not only coming from the past,
they are coming from an earlier type of world-formation.
Imagine them emerging from, say, an aquatic world.
Analyst and analysand are on a dinghy, neither really
knows the seas. For a while you just sit in the dinghy and
drift along; then, wonk!, a huge tentacle whacks the boat
and fastens to the side. With associations and interpretations one can follow the tentacle down for a bit; but then,
wonk!, another tentacle hits the other side. One contin-

---

21. Loewald (1960, pp. 248–249).
22. Hartley (2002).

ues on in this way until an octopus is suddenly hugging the boat. This is the transference neurosis. A good analyst is like a fisherman: he knows that if he waits with analytic patience, the octopus will eventually be clamoring to get on deck.

But how do you bring the aquatic world and terrestrial world together? That is the problem of the transference neurosis. It is a weird kind of world-historical crisis—a clash of two alien worlds, one from the archaic past, in which each doesn't really know the other exists. The analytic situation is structured so that it is likely to attract all sorts of transference connections piecemeal. The unconscious is throwing up connections; these are the ghosts, the heirs of an archaic past. They establish distorted and distorting connections between the two worlds. One might think of them as "trans-world heir lines."[23] But if the analysis flourishes, there comes a point where *the worldiness* of the unconscious bursts forth into conscious awareness with all of its living vibrancy. We are no longer concerned with uncovering the meaning of this or that transference relationship; rather, it is the world as a whole that opens up.

Let us go back for the last time to Mr. A. and Dr. L. There is a spasm of coughing and

> he suddenly became intensely angry with me, saying, "Do I want to tell you to fuck off!" He then began cough-

---

23. This phrase is due to the philosopher David Kaplan, who used it in the context of modal semantics.

ing uncontrollably for several minutes, finally leaving
the office for a minute to go to the bathroom for a drink
of water. Returning to the couch, he asked, "Why would
I want to tell you to fuck off? You haven't done anything
but been here."

I said, "Maybe that's why."

"Yes, you're the doctor," he replied. "Why haven't
you cured me? I've been waiting for you to fix me."

This was the moment when Mr. A. experienced the
full intensity of his hostility toward me in the waning
months of the analysis.[24]

What makes this moment so important is not merely that
Mr. A. is able to experience his hostility toward the analyst, but that he is able to experience his hostility *as he
grasps its world-structuring role*. In the repeated coughing
fits, the ghost is, as it were, clearing his throat. He finally
gets to break through into speech, "Do I want to tell you
to fuck off!" Even in the outburst, one can still see compromise formation and defense: "Do I want to" is a phrase
that can be used ambiguously to ask a question and declare a heartfelt wish. Still, here we have a ghost yelling
"fuck off!" But, as we've learned, ghosts bring messages
from another world. If we really understand the message,
we've got to understand more than "fuck off!" (though
that's a start); we have to understand the world from
which "fuck off!" makes sense. Of course, this other world
is an archaic world, its structure is inchoate, so as Mr. A.

---

24. Levenson (1998), op. cit., p. 858.

charts its structure he will be adding structure; this is what is involved in bringing the unconscious up into conscious, linguistic formulation. Mr. A. has moved from a coughing spasm to an expletive, from an expletive to a well-formulated question, and, with the help of his analyst, from a question to irony. He is now at the stage of his analysis where he can give himself the meaning of that other world: "You've never done anything but been here." This is a "point of attachment" where two worlds meet. Seeing the irony of that remark enables Mr. A. not only to explore both worlds, but also to explore the dynamic relations between the two. On the conscious level, the phrase tries to sum up the analytic relationship as a whole, as it is coming to an end. It is meant as an expression of gratitude, and it places the analytic relation in the context of a larger world of social relations. Unlike this relation or that where someone wanted something or other from me, unlike this or that relationship where someone let me down when I've needed them, you've just been there for me. This one utterance consciously places the analyst in the universe of Mr. A.'s social relations.

But, then, so does the unconscious meaning. "I've been coming every day for five years like a dutiful analysand [son, friend, lover, husband] and all you've done is sit on your ass! I came to you because I was in trouble, and you haven't done a fucking thing. Now you're going to abandon me (just like my mother, father, friend, mentor, wife, sibling did), and I'm going to have to say 'thank you very much'. Well, fuck off!" All we actually hear are the last two words. Again the analysand

is trying to sum up the meaning of the entire relationship, but he does so by placing it in a very different world
of meanings. This world is structured by disappointment
and fury. There are furious ghosts, ghosts of Mr. A.'s past,
furious that he did not get the love and attention he felt
he deserved. They are crying out that the world is unfair,
it's disappointing, and that people are unresponsive, they
don't care.

Like every neurotic, Mr. A. has in effect lived his life
between two worlds, without really knowing the nature
of either. The underworld has remained opaque to him,
but it has also exerted a distorting influence on the world
he consciously inhabits. Now he can start to bring those
worlds together in new ways. He can see, for instance,
that while he genuinely feels gratitude to his analyst for
being there, he has also used his gratitude as a means of
covering over angry feelings. He has used authority figures as external superegos, means of tamping his anger
down. As a result, the anger disappeared from conscious
awareness, but the world was now structured around
obsequiousness and excessive gratitude to authority figures, combined with breakthrough experiences of resent-
ment and distrust that he didn't really understand.

We can now see more clearly why irony is so important for therapeutic action. For an appropriate irony—
"You've never done anything but been here"—is the
perfect vehicle for traveling up and down the "heir lines"
of transference. In its irony it allows the analysand to
explore both worlds, and to bring them together. For
the irony establishes a completely different way of bring-

ing unconscious and conscious together. Before the interpretation, the unconscious had brutally slapped down its connections: the analyst is the punishing authority, the analysand the cringing and resentful ego. These are the heirs of the unconscious, the ghosts that are still inhabiting the analytic present. Bringing out the irony establishes a different kind of connection—a gentle connection that runs through meaning. The analysand can now explore the world from which this ghost arose, and in so doing place him back in his context. It is in this way that "the ghosts of the unconscious are laid and led to rest as ancestors whose power is taken over and transformed into a newer intensity of present life."

At the end of the *Symposium*, Plato's great disquisition on the therapeutic possibilities of love, Socrates says enigmatically that poets ought to be equally good at writing tragedy and comedy. It is irony that brings the pathos and the comedy of the analytic situation to light. It is utterly sad that at this late stage of his life Mr. A. is still in an angry cringe before Dr. L. That he can now leave it makes the situation truly hilarious.

6

Revocation

How is one to end a book on therapeutic action? Or, rather, what would a therapeutic ending be? With a recovered memory? Here it again seems useful to take a step back to a moment in Western intellectual and emotional life just before the introduction of psychoanalysis. The great therapeutic book, written in the generation before Freud, is *Concluding Unscientific Postscript* by Johannes Climacus. This book is written in the midst of Christian life, and its official topic, the manifest content, is the difficulty involved in becoming a Christian. This may seem an alien topic for secular readers today. All the more so for psychoanalysts who have been persuaded by Freud's critique of religious belief. Still, no matter what your religious orientation or lack of orientation, we cut ourselves off from our own past if we simply disregard the great works of nineteenth century Europe. For this is the soil from which psychoanalysis grew. Whatever one's current religious belief or lack of belief or hostility to belief, it is antipsychoanalytic to refuse to look back to one's heritage. Here I am not interested in any particular influence on Freud the individual, but rather in a diagnosis of the spiritual climate of his time.

Climacus' ending is bizarre: he revokes his entire book. What could this possibly mean?[1] Climacus, for his part, certainly takes the revocation to be essential to the therapeutic action of his book. In an appendix entitled "For an Understanding with the Reader," he says, "The undersigned, Johannes Climacus, who has written this book, does not give himself out to be a Christian; *he is completely taken up with the thought how difficult it must be to be a Christian;* . . . In the aloofness of the experiment the whole work has to do with me myself, solely and simply with me." He then goes on to quote himself from the introduction, reminding the reader that he was warned at the beginning:

> "I, Johannes Climacus, now thirty years of age, born in Copenhagen, a plain man like the common run of them, have heard tell of a highest good in prospect, which is called eternal blessedness, and that Christianity will bestow this upon me on condition of adhering to it—now I ask how I am to become a Christian" (cf. the Introduction). I ask only for my own sake, yes, certainly that I do,

---

1. For marvelous discussions of Kierkegaard and issues related to revocation, see James Conant (1992, 1996).

or rather I have asked this question, for that indeed is
the content of the whole work.[2]

On the face of it, one might think that the revocation is a reaffirmation of the fact that the therapeutic
action embodied in his book is for him, and for him
alone. At the beginning of the book he says this is his
own therapy, and the revocation at the end ostensibly
reaffirms that writing the book has been for him and him
alone. But then why publish the book? Is Climacus not
behaving like the religious leader he mocks, the one who
teaches that a religious figure should have no disciples?
For, after all, the revocation begins in an appendix that
itself begins on page 545 of my English translation. The
reader who has slogged through the previous 544 pages
of philosophy and theology, as I have, might be forgiven
for thinking: Does this really have nothing to do with me?
Am I nothing more than the Other in the presence of
whom Climacus has gone through his own private therapy?
What is Climacus doing such that he wants to suggest to
me that that is my role?

Climacus says that he is a "humorist in private practice." He pictures himself as author and audience of his
own jokes. (At first this may seem strange but, if you think
about it, a good many joke-tellers are precisely that.)
Climacus is someone who has written the book for his
own amusement. Or, at least, so he says. But why, then,

---

2. Kierkegaard (1846), op. cit., p. 545 (my emphasis). The quoted
sentence from introduction also appears on p. 19.

does he say that? If the book really is for his own amusement, why did he feel the need to tack on an appendix
entitled, "For an Understanding with the Reader"? It
seems that the understanding he is seeking with his
reader is that he has written the book for himself! Imagine the termination phase of an analysis in which the
analysand keeps reassuring the analyst that she has really gone through the analysis for herself. The analyst
ought to wonder what all this reassurance is about. Indeed, if the analyst doesn't wonder, then they are both
ensnared in a comic performance. The analysand is re-
citing the dogma of antidogmatism—"I've done this
analysis for myself!"—and the analyst is tacitly congratulating himself, by congratulating her. To paraphrase that
famous line from *My Fair Lady*: "I think she's got it! By
George, she's got it! Now once again, who's this analysis
for?" "For me! For me! . . ."

Climacus assures us that he is a humorist in private
practice. Might this not be an ironic performance that is
also utter earnestness? That is, in assuring us that he is in
private practice, he makes himself ludicrous, but he simultaneously frees us from participating in a comic duet.
The performance is so ridiculous—ridiculous in our
eyes—that we are thereby liberated from the routine. In
particular, we are going to be freed from the temptation
to say, "Psst. The Master teaches us that it's very difficult
to become a Christian, and above all you can't become a
Christian by learning his teaching. Be careful about passing this along!" This might have been the position of a
reader at the end of the book, before the appendix. But

by going on to revoke the entire book, by insisting he is in private practice, however ridiculous that assertion may be after 544 published pages of goings on, he effectively puts himself into private practice. He is a comic sacrificial lamb. In ostensibly cutting himself off from the reader, he enables the reader to separate from him.

Climacus describes his act this way:

> As in Catholic books, especially those of an earlier age, one finds at the back of the volume a note which informs the reader that everything is to be understood conformably with the doctrine of the Holy Catholic Mother Church—so what I write contains also a piece of information to the effect that everything is to be so understood that it is understood to be revoked, and the book has not only a Conclusion but a Revocation.[3]

This passage is dripping with irony. Climacus, if he were able to become a Christian, would no doubt become a Protestant, so the genre that he mentions is for him a specifically Catholic form of decadence. If the body of one's text is blasphemy, can one really get off the hook by saying in an appendix that everything is to be understood as in conformity with the doctrines of the Church? If Galileo had appended such a disclaimer to his *Dialogue of the Great World Systems*, would he thereby have brought his teachings into conformity with the Church? What kind of a "revocation" could such a performance

---

3. Kierkegaard (1846), op. cit., p. 547.

possibly bring about? If Climacus likens his own act of revocation to this kind of performance, isn't he thereby undermining his own act? Does Climacus, in the very act of revoking his own work, undermine his revocation?

Yet earnestness is also present. Climacus writes that what he writes also contains "a piece of information"—namely, the information that everything is to be understood as revoked. But by now we readers ought to be wary of "pieces of information." For the crucial issue cannot be *what* pieces of information we have, but *how we live* with them. If the "revocation" is only a piece of information, it deserves the skeptical scare-quotes I am giving it: for it is "revocation" in name only.[4] It seems that Climacus is trying at once to put on display both the gesture and its emptiness. Climacus tells us as much himself: "So then the book is superfluous; let no one therefore take the pains to appeal to it as an authority;

---

4. By way of analogy, consider the marvelous article by Lewis Carroll, "What the Tortoise Said to Achilles" (*Mind*, 1895). In it the Tortoise challenges Achilles to a logical race: Achilles is to get the Tortoise to move from the premises **A** and **If A, then B** to the conclusion **B**. The Tortoise agrees to both of the premises. Indeed, they are valuable "pieces of information." But he can't see how to get to the conclusion. For doesn't he need another premise? Namely, **If A and If A, then B, then B**. Achilles lets him have that premise, an additional piece of information. But still the Tortoise can't see how to get to **B**. Doesn't he need another piece of information, viz., **If A and If A, then B, then B, then B**? And so on. One of the many lessons of this marvelous tale is that "pieces of information" on their own are not by themselves going to force a particular way of living with them.

for he who thus appeals to it has *eo ipso* misunderstood it."[5] So even if the reader appeals to the "piece of information" that the entire book is revoked, hasn't he thereby misunderstood it? But, then, what is this revocation? If we cannot appeal to it, what are we to make of it?

The reader knows all along that Johannes Climacus is a pseudonymous author. He is not a mere pen name for Kierkegaard, but he never quite inhabited flesh and blood either. Although these are the last words of Climacus, they are not the last word. After the *Concluding Unscientific Postscript* concludes, after this appendix in which the book is revoked, there is, as I said at the beginning of this work, "A First and Last Declaration," and this three-and-a-half page document is signed by S. Kierkegaard. In it, Kierkegaard declares that he is the author *"as people would call it"* of the *Concluding Unscientific Postscript*, as well as the other pseudonymous works. But, he continues:

> My pseudonymity . . . has not had a casual ground in my person . . . but it has an *essential* ground in the character of the *production*. . . . What is written therefore is in fact mine, but only in so far as I put into the mouth of the poetically actual individuality whom I *produced*, his life-view expressed in audible lines. For my relation is even more external than that of a poet, who poetizes characters, and yet in the preface is himself the author. For I am impersonal, or personal in the second person, a

---

5. Kierkegaard (1846), op. cit., p. 546.

souffleur who has poetically produced the *authors,* whose preface in turn is their own production, as are even their own names. So in the pseudonymous works there is not a single word which is mine, I have no opinion about these works except as a third person, no knowledge of their meaning except as a reader, not the remotest private relation to them, since such a thing is impossible in the case of a doubly reflected communication. One single word of mine uttered personally in my own name would be an instance of presumptuous self-forgetfulness, and dialectically viewed it would incur with one word the guilt of annihilating the pseudonyms."[6]

OK, so we are dealing with a pseudonymous author, not with a mere pen name. Does not this put us in a position analogous to an analyst listening to an analysand? For a reader confronted with an author he knows to be pseudonymous needs to figure out not merely *what* this author is saying, but *who the author is* who is saying it. Who is this Climacus who is saying these things to me? The aim is not to discover what Kierkegaard really meant to say, as though he were hiding behind the pseudonym. Nothing so cutesy is going on. Yet, knowing that Johannes Climacus is a poetical creation, we are in a position to ask about the poetical meaning of the alleged revocation.

Similarly, an analysand typically presents him- or herself as a poetical creation. The analyst must perpetually listen not merely to what the analysand is saying, but

---

6. Kierkegaard (1846), op. cit., p. 551.

also with the question, Who is this who is saying this to me? The analysand may come with all sorts of fantasies about getting over her past, getting rid of emotional baggage, of being able to start a new kind of intimate life, and so on. Yet there is reason to suspect that any alleged revocation of the past will be utterly entangled in the pseudonymous author whose past it is. Psychoanalysis needs to be able to expose the pseudo-revocations of the pseudonymous authors who spend time on our couches.

Climacus is a master at exposing the hypocrisy, the false starts, the illusions of the Christianity of his day. It is a stunning exposition of the spiritual malaise of an age. Official Christianity, what Climacus calls Christendom, was not entirely moribund, but it had become too easy. One symptom, for Climacus, was the facility with which philosophically minded authors could pronounce on the spiritual meaning of the age. Thus Climacus meant his revocation as a healthy (and ironic) antidote to any such solemn pronouncement. "Let no one put himself out to say that the book is entirely superfluous and quite irrelevant to the times—unless in the end he has to say something, for in that case he pronounces the wished-for judgment, which indeed I have already passed upon the author."[7] Climacus thus pronounces his own work as "entirely superfluous," "quite irrelevant to the times."

There is a deep meaning here, embedded in the comic gesture. Climacus is reminding us by his own example, that when it comes to Christianity we ought to

---

7. Kierkegaard (1846), op. cit., p. 545.

spend less time paying attention to the pronouncements of supposed religious or philosophical guides, and look to our own souls. In the revocation, Climacus subverts the idea that his book can be used as another philosophical guide, subverts the idea that he is another wise man pronouncing on the meaning of the age. The revocation insists that the book is nothing more than his own spiritual exercise. Yet, in so insisting, he shifts the literary genre. Consider, by way of analogy, another great philosophical work, Descartes's *Meditations*. The *Meditations* are not trying to convince another to adopt any particular beliefs. Rather, they purport to be the journey of a solitary ego, an I, on the path of secure knowledge. If a reader wants, any I can take up that path. It is an intellectual journey that can be imitated, and in so doing, any I can go through the "therapeutic action" for itself. In a similar vein, Climacus' revocation is meant to bring this book back to an exercise for himself alone; yet it simultaneously provides a model that anyone could imitate for himself or herself alone. As Climacus puts it with ironic understatement, "To write a book and revoke it is something else than not writing it at all."[8]

And yet, and yet. However incisive the critiques of his society, however intimate the act of revocation, the reader arrives at an uncanny sense that something pathological is also being put on display. We are in a world of compromise formation. We may not yet know what the compromises are, but we readers have become, almost

---

8. Kierkegaard (1846), op. cit., p. 548.

imperceptibly, hermeneutically suspicious of our author. What is he up to? What we come to suspect is that although he is a master in explaining to us how Christianity has become too easy, in his life he puts on display how, for him, it has become too difficult. Not that any of his specific criticisms are wrong, but why does he need to keep telling us about them? Indeed, if his revocation really is an act by which he declares that he is really only talking to himself, why does he need to keep telling himself? Climacus tells us that "he is completely taken up with the thought how difficult it must be to be a Christian," and after 550 pages of going on, we believe him! What we, the readers, slowly come to see is that whatever the genuine difficulties involved in becoming a Christian, for Climacus these difficulties are serving to prevent him ever becoming one. Climacus is wallowing in difficulty.

Compare the analysis of a high-functioning neurotic. There will typically be incisive critiques of the immediate social scene, of parents, siblings, friends, colleagues. But, as one listens, one wonders, what are these critiques for? However accurate they may be in what they say, what pathology is being put on display in how they are said? Think of young Dora's stunning accounts of the hypocrisies of the adult world that surrounded her. Isn't her central criticism that her father, Frau K., and Herr K. are all making it too easy on themselves? Dora is convinced that there is something more difficult involved in life well lived, and yet pathology infects her own sense of difficulty. Freud's self-acknowledged failure in this case can be put like this: although he was attentive to the difficulties Dora described (the what), he was obtuse to the difficulties she had in living (the how). One might say that the category of becoming a woman in relation to men and other women was as difficult for Dora as the category of becoming a Christian was for Climacus. In other words, in their idiosyncratic ways, both were stuck in (a pathological sense of) difficulty. As a result of Freud's therapeutic failure, Dora brought about an epoch-making revocation of her own.

It would be tempting as a literary conceit to end this book by offering a revocation of my own. Couldn't I offer this last chapter as a revocation of the entire book? No I cannot. As I said at the beginning, this book is written to a significant extent for myself, to continue the process of deepening myself as a psychoanalyst. But it is also written for others. While it is written in a style that I hope will encourage the reader to play with the concepts, it is also the case that I think that what I said about subjectivity and objectivity, internalization, drives, and transference is true. Thus I have not had to construct a pseudonymous author to write this book; I am writing this book in my own person. Thus to enact a revocation would be worse than an empty gesture, it would be false.

What I can do, though, and what seems analytically appropriate, is to offer a loose association, and associations to that association. From *revocation* to *re-vocation*. The activity in this book is meant to recall us to our vocation as psychoanalysts. It is a recalling to our calling. Here the issue is not, à la Climacus, that one should forever be taken up with how difficult it is to become a psychoanalyst. The secular-therapeutic equivalent of Climacus would be a person who felt he could never become a psychoanalyst because he was so absorbed in all the difficulties of really being one. He would be someone who was brilliant at exposing the hypocrisies of the psychoanalytic profession, but who himself remained stuck in difficulty; a person who could never quite enter the promised land, the subjective category of psychoanalyst. Here, by contrast, we begin already inside the life of analysis, and the examination of difficulties is part of our never-ending process of deepening ourselves as analysts. Rather than obstacles to becoming a psychoanalyst, these are the intellectual challenges by which we reaffirm our subjective identity. Thus it does not seem far-fetched or false to think of this book not only as about therapeutic action but as part of the continuing therapeutic action of psychoanalysis.

Acknowledgments

This book grows out of a weekly conversation with Hans Loewald that spanned about six years. The book *is* its own acknowledgment. There is a philosophical conversation going on at the University of Chicago, and those who have ever participated in one know how special that is. My colleagues at that unique intellectual institution, the Committee on Social Thought, have encouraged me to think in new ways about age-old problems. My colleagues in the philosophy department allow me the joy of knowing I live in a neighborhood where philosophy is alive. In particular, I should like to thank James Conant and John Haugeland for extended conversations about Kierkegaard and Heidegger, respectively. Thanks to the members of the seminar on *Concluding Unscientific Postscript* (conducted with James Conant) for helping me get clear on what is meant by irony. David Carlson and Braxton McKee, two gifted analysts and colleagues at the

Western New England Institute for Psychoanalysis, both of whom knew Loewald well, read through the manuscript and offered invaluable comments. So did Michael Moskowitz, who first proposed the idea to me of writing an extended essay on therapeutic action. Neither of us understood what that one remark would lead to. Stacy Hague, my editor at Other Press, has been an unfailing help as we saw this manuscript through. My dear friend Jane Levin, who reads all my work in draft and serves as my intelligent reader, helped me again, as always. But, above all, I am indebted to my daughter Sophia and to my wife Gabriel, not only for their extraordinarily helpful comments on a previous draft, but for being there.

References

Aristotle. *The Complete Works of Aristotle: The Revised Oxford Translation*, ed. J. Barnes. Princeton: Princeton University Press, 1984.

Bettelheim, B. (1983). *Freud and Man's Soul.* New York: Knopf.

Carroll, L. (1895). What the tortoise said to Achilles. *Mind*, Vol. 4, pp. 278–280.

Conant, J. (1992). Kierkegaard, Wittgenstein and Nonsense. In *Pursuits of Reason,* ed. T. Cohen, P. Guyer, and H. Putnam, pp. 195–224. Lubbock, TX: Texas Tech University Press.

——— (1996). Putting two and two together: Kierkegaard, Wittgenstein and the point of view for their work as authors. In *The Grammar of Religious Belief,* ed. D. Z. Phillips, pp. 248–331. New York: St. Martins Press.

Dor, J. (1999). *The Clinical Lacan.* New York: Other Press.

Fink, B. (1997). *A Clinical Introduction to Lacanian Psychoanalysis: Theory and Technique.* Cambridge, MA: Harvard University Press.

Fowler, H. W. (1926). *A Dictionary of Modern English Usage.* Oxford: Clarendon Press.

Freud, S. (1893–1895). Studies on hysteria. *Standard Edition* 2:1–305.

———— (1895). Project for a scientific psychology. *Standard Edition* 1:283–397.

———— (1896). The aetiology of hysteria. *Standard Edition* 3: 189–221.

———— (1900). The interpretation of dreams. *Standard Edition* 4/5:1–626.

———— (1905a). Fragment of an analysis of a case of hysteria. *Standard Edition* 7:3–122.

———— (1905b). Three essays on the theory of sexuality. *Standard Edition* 7:125–243.

———— (1911). Psycho-analytic notes on an autobiographical account of a case of paranoia. *Standard Edition* 12:3–82.

———— (1914). On narcissism: an introduction. *Standard Edition* 14:67–102.

———— (1915). Instincts and their vicissitudes. *Standard Edition* 14:105–140.

———— (1920). Beyond the pleasure principle. *Standard Edition* 18:3–64.

———— (1921). Group psychology and the analysis of the ego. *Standard Edition* 18:67–143.

———— (1923). The ego and the id. *Standard Edition* 19:3–66.

———— (1924). The resistances of psycho-analysis. *Standard Edition* 19:213–224.

———— (1925). An autobiographical study. *Standard Edition* 20:3–70.

———— (1929). Civilization and its discontents. *Standard Edition* 21:59–145.

———— (1932). New introductory lectures on psycho-analysis. *Standard Edition* 22:3–182.

———— (1937). Analysis terminable and interminable. *Standard Edition* 23:211–253.

———— (1940). An outline of psycho-analysis. *Standard Edition* 23:141–207.

———— (1953). *On Aphasia.* New York: International Universities Press.

S. Freud, and Jung, C. J. (1974). *The Freud/Jung Letters.* ed. W. McGuire, trans. R. Manheim and R. F. C. Hull. Princeton: Princeton University Press.

Gay, P. (1998). *Freud: A Life for Our Times.* New York: W. W. Norton.

Gray, P. (1982). "Developmental lag" in the evolution of technique for psychoanalysis of neurotic conflict. *Journal of the American Psychoanalytical Association* 30:621–655. Reprinted in Gray (1994), pp. 29–61.

———— (1987). Analysis of the ego's inhibiting superego activities. In Gray (1994), pp. 105–127. Originally published under the title: On the technique of the analysis of the superego—an introduction. *Psychoanalytic Quarterly* 56:130–154.

———— (1994). *The Ego and Analysis of Defense.* Northvale, NJ: Jason Aronson.

Gurewich, J. F. (1999). *Lacan and the New Wave in American Psychoanalysis.* New York: Other Press.

Hartley, L.P. (2002). *The Go-Between.* New York: New York Review of Books.

Haugeland, J. (1998). Truth and rule-following. In *Having Thought: Essays in the Metaphysics of Mind,* pp. 305–361. Cambridge: Harvard University Press.

———— (2000). Truth and finitude: Heidegger's transcendental existentialism. In *Heidegger, Authenticity and Modernity: Essays in Honor of Herbert L. Dreyfus,* Vol. 1, ed. M. Wrathall and J. Malpas, pp. 43–77. Cambridge: MIT Press.

Heidegger, M. (1927). *Being and Time.* Albany: State University Press of New York, 1996.

Joseph, B. (1989). Transference: the total situation. In *Psychic Equilibrium and Psychic Change: Selected Papers of Betty Joseph*, ed. M. Feldman and E. B. Spillius, pp. 156–167. London and New York: Routledge.

Kant, I. (1787). *Critique of Pure Reason*, trans. N. K. Smith. New York: St. Martin's Press, 1965.

Kierkegaard, S. (1846). *Concluding Unscientific Postscript to the Philosophical Fragments: A Mimic-Pathetic-Dialectic Composition: An Existential Contribution*, by Johannes Climacus. Responsible for publication: S. Kierkegaard. Trans. D. F. Swenson and W. Lowrie. Princeton: Princeton University Press, 1941.

—— (1960). *The Diary of Soren Kierkegaard*, ed. P. Rhode. New York: Citadel Press, 1993.

Lacan, J. (1985). Intervention on transference. In *Dora's Case: Freud-Hysteria-Feminism*, ed. C. Bernheimer and C. Kahane, pp. 92–104. New York: Columbia University Press.

—— (1987). *Four Fundamental Concepts of Psychoanalysis*. New York, Penguin.

—— (1993). *The Seminar of Jacques Lacan, Book III: The Psychoses 1955–1956*. New York: W. W. Norton.

Laplanche, J. (1985). *Life and Death in Psychoanalysis*. Baltimore: Johns Hopkins University Press.

Levenson, L. (1998). Superego defense analysis in the termination phase. *Journal of the American Psychoanalytic Association* 46:847–866.

Little, W., Fowler, H. W., Coulson, J., and Onions, C. T. eds. (1972). *The Shorter Oxford English Dictionary on Historical Principles*, 3rd ed. Oxford: Oxford University Press.

Loewald, H. (1951). Ego and reality. *International Journal of Psycho-Analysis* 32:10–18. Reprinted in Loewald (2000), pp. 3–20.

—— (1960). On the therapeutic action of psychoanalysis.

International Journal of Psycho-Analysis 41:16–33. Reprinted in Loewald (2000), pp. 221–256.

———— (1970). Psychoanalytic theory and psychoanalytic process. *Psychoanalytic Study of the Child* 25:45–68. New York: International Universities Press. Reprinted in Loewald (2000), pp. 277–301.

———— (1971a). Discussion: Max Schur, "The Regulatory Principles of Mental Functioning." In Loewald (2000), pp. 58–68.

———— (1971b). The transference neurosis: comments on the concept and on the phenomenon. *Journal of the American Psychoanalytic Association* 19:54–66. Reprinted in Loewald (2000), pp. 302–325.

———— (1973). On internalization. *International Journal of Psycho-Analysis* 54:9–17. Reprinted with additions in Loewald (2000), pp. 69–86.

———— (2000). *The Essential Loewald: Collected Papers and Monographs*. Hagerstown, MD: University Publishing Group.

Mathelin, C. (1999). *Lacanian Psychotherapy with Children: The Broken Piano*. New York: Other Press.

McDowell, J. (1994). *Mind and World*. Cambridge, MA: Harvard University Press.

———— (1998). *Mind, Value and Reality*. Cambridge, MA: Harvard University Press.

Nasio, J.-D. (1998a). *Five Lessons on the Psychoanalytic Theory of Jacques Lacan*. Albany: State University of New York Press.

———— (1998b). *Hysteria from Freud to Lacan: The Splendid Child of Psychoanalysis*. New York: Other Press.

Pally, R. (2000). *The Mind-Brain Relationship*. London and New York: Karnac Books.

Plato. *The Republic*, trans. T. Griffith. Cambridge: Cambridge University Press. 2000.

————. *Symposium.* In Plato, *Complete Works,* ed. J. M. Cooper, pp. 457–505. Indianapolis: Hackett.

Proust, M. (1913). *In Search of Lost Time,* trans. C. K. Scott Moncrieff, T. Kilmartin, and D. J. Enright. New York: Modern Library, 1992.

Rizzuto, A.-M. (1993). Freud's speech apparatus and spontaneous speech. *International Journal of Psycho-Analysis* 74: 113–127.

Schafer, R. (1970). The psychoanalytic vision of reality. *International Journal of Psycho-Analysis* 51:279–297.

Schreber, D. P. (1903). *Memoirs of My Nervous Illness,* trans. I. Macalpine and R. A. Hunter. Cambridge, MA: Harvard University Press, 1988.

Solms, M. (1997). What is consciousness? *Journal of the American Psychoanalytic Association* 45:681–778.

Solms, M., and Saling, M. (1986). On psychoanalysis and neuroscience: Freud's attitude to the localization tradition. *International Journal of Psycho-Analysis* 67:397–416.

Solms, M., and Turnbull, O. (2002). *The Brain and the Inner World: An Introduction to the Neuroscience of Subjective Experience.* New York: Other Press.

Stein, M. H. (1985). Irony in psychoanalysis. *Journal of the American Philosophical Association* 33:35–57.

Stoppard, T. (1972). *Jumpers.* London: Faber and Faber.

Strachey, J. (1934). The nature of the therapeutic action of psychoanalysis. *International Journal of Psycho-Analysis* 50: 275–292.

Sulloway, F. J. (1979). *Freud, Biologist of the Mind: Beyond the Psychoanalytic Legend.* New York: Basic Books.

Vanier, A. (2000). *Lacan.* New York: Other Press.

Verhaeghe, P. (2001). *Beyond Gender: From Subject to Drive.* New York: Other Press.

Vlastos, G. (1991). *Socrates: Ironist and Moral Philosopher.* New York and Cambridge: Cambridge University Press.

Williams, B. (1985). *Ethics and the Limits of Philosophy*. Cambridge, MA: Harvard University Press.

Žižek, S. (1989). *The Sublime Object of Ideology*. London and New York: Verso.

Zupancic, A. (2000). *Ethics of the Real: Kant, Lacan*. New York and London: Verso.

Index